JAMES C. SCHAAP

NO KIDDING, GOD

DEVOTIONS FOR TODAY'S FAMILY

JAMES C. SCHAAP

NO KIDDING, GOD

DEVOTIONS ▾ FOR TODAY'S FAMILY

CRCPUBLICATIONS
Grand Rapids, Michigan

Printed in the United States of America.

Library of Congress Cataloging-in-Publication Data
Schaap, James C., 1948-
No Kidding, God/James C. Schaap.
p. cm.—(Devotions for today's family)
1. Bible. O.T. Psalms—Meditations.
2. Family—Prayer-books and devotions—English.
I. Title. II. Series.
BS1430.4.S33 1990   89-48197
242'.5—dc20   CIP

ISBN 0-930265-86-6

CONTENTS

PREFACE

Between our public praise on Sunday mornings and our personal times of Bible reading, meditation, and prayer lies a third category of worship—family devotions. In some Christian circles, families maintain a strong tradition of gathering regularly before God—before or after meals or before bedtime—for Bible reading and prayer.

Family devotions preserve family faith, teach children how to worship, and provide a time when parents and children can talk together about what they believe and whom they serve. At a time when the family seems in crisis, bent and torn by social changes, such shared worship times can be vital to a family's stability and health.

Most families appreciate some guide to structure their Bible reading and spark discussion. With small children parents often use a Bible storybook. But for families who have older children or children of a wide range of ages, finding appropriate material that appeals to all is more difficult.

Devotions for Today's Family is a series of family devotional books written at the middle-school reading level. Each devotion suggests a Scripture reading and a prayer. Between these, it either tells a story or reflects on something in the theme or Scripture in a personal and vivid way that makes the ideas come alive and challenges family members to think and talk about their faith.

No Kidding, God is the title of this devotional book. In it the author writes on some of the Psalms—well-known and well-loved hymns of faith like Psalm 23, "The Lord is my shepherd," and Psalm 42, "As the deer pants for streams of water." The words, themes, and ideas of these psalms come alive through these meditations.

James C. Schaap, author of *No Kidding, God*, is a professor of English at Dordt College in Sioux Center, Iowa. Prolific writer of short stories and authentic reflector of the Reformed ethos in a midwestern context, Schaap is above all a Christian who thinks deeply and writes wisely about his own faith experience. His published works include *CRC Family Portrait*, stories about ordinary Christians; *Intermission*, a popular book of devotionals for teenagers; and *Someone's Singing, Lord*, another book in the present series.

No Kidding, God is offered with the prayer that it may help your family to worship in a way that will deepen the faith of every family member.

Harvey A. Smit
Editor in Chief
Education Department
CRC Publications

PSALM 22

HONESTY I

When he finally couldn't live with himself anymore, Matt went to Mr. Adkins. Everybody knew Adkins was an okay teacher.

"Let's just say," Matt told him, "that this kid's got a friend who picked up something the kid wanted really bad—you know? But the kid doesn't know how the friend got it—"

"He figures the friend stole it, I bet," Adkins said.

"Let's just say that," Matt said. "I mean, let's just make up something here, like a for-instance."

Adkins was crouched on his desk like a toad. He'd been standing on the desk to reach the thumbtacks at the top of the bulletin board when Matt walked in.

"So you want to know what the kid ought to do if he knows his friend stole the goods?"

"Something like that," Matt said, looking down at the papers on the desk. The truth was that Matt had gotten three tapes from Whitney, a girl who was rich enough to buy them. But she hadn't—he knew it. She'd probably grabbed them off a store counter because he'd told her he wanted a Mama's Boys album. That's all he'd said. Two days later, she had three.

"Maybe the kid ought to ask the friend if he stole them," Adkins said. "Nothing beats honesty."

"But the thing is, she—" Matt said, without thinking.

"Ah, the plot thickens," Adkins said, raising a finger. "The crook's a female."

Matt turned and growled. Adkins was making fun of him. "This ain't no game," Matt said, walking away. "I'm serious."

Just like that Adkins launched himself off the desk and landed on both feet, his hands on Matt's shoulders. "Then don't beat around the bush," he said. "All day I've been playing games with kids. Now talk to me."

Matt felt like he had to trust Adkins. There was just something about him.

"All right," Matt said, ready to talk but determined to protect Whitney. "There's this girl I know. Anyway, she gave me three tapes—just gave them to me, man."

"You think she stole them?"

Matt nodded his head.

"Ask her," Adkins said. "Ask her right out."

Matt knew he couldn't do that. No way could he just go right up to Whitney and ask her if she'd lifted those tapes. No way. "I can't," he said. "You don't just ask somebody if she's a stinking thief."

"Then pray about it," Adkins advised.

"Get serious," Matt told him.

"I am," Adkins said.

"So what do I ask God? 'Please tell me if she stole them tapes, Jesus'?" He put a hand on the desk to steady himself.

"You don't have to ask him anything. Just talk to him," Adkins said. "Talk to God. Tell him everything."

"You don't just *talk* to God," Matt said. "You ask him for junk."

"Why?" Adkins asked.

"I don't know. How do you expect me to know?"

"Look," Adkins said, "you want my advice? Ask the girl if she stole the tapes. But whatever you do, pray about it. Tell it to God just like you're telling it to me. Talk to him. Tell him the truth." He swung his leg over a desk and reached for the second row of pictures on his bulletin board.

"She's a friend, you know? She gave me these tapes, and I don't know if I should keep 'em."

"Tell *him* that."

"And if I ask her if she stole them, she'll drop me like a bad habit."

"Tell him that too," Adkins said. "Tell God everything. He just wants to hear. He wants your trust. Be honest."

"God?" Matt said.

"He's alive. He'll listen."

"You telling the truth?"

"Honest to God," Adkins told him, smiling. "Honest to God. Hey," he continued, "do me a favor and scrape that spitwad off the buffalo there."

Not five minutes later Matt started home across the field beside the new school, walking along the fence where trash collected in the mesh. It was a dirty world, he thought.

Ask her, Adkins had said. Honesty's the best policy and all that. Sure, Matt thought. Like so much hooey. You just don't talk to people like that. You just don't say, "Hey, you steal those tapes, Whit?" You don't talk to anyone like that, he thought, and not to God either. No way.

He'd have to figure out something himself, Matt decided. Adkins was an all right guy, but that didn't mean you could believe everything he said.

Lord, sometimes it seems as if you're way up there beyond us. But you aren't. You want to know us and everything we're thinking about. Help us to be honest with you. Help us to talk to you about everything. You're our Savior, our Lord, and our Friend. Amen.

A WORM AND NOT A MAN

....
Psalm 22:1-8

My nephew Mike claims that the guy who took his sister to the prom is a worm. Heidi doesn't deny it. She growls a little when he says it, but she claims the really nice guy she wanted to ask her didn't, so it was a case of go with the worm or stay home. She decided on the worm.

Stuck up on the refrigerator is a picture of Mike with his date, a picture some photographer took right there at the prom. The girl is blonde, and she looks like something worth crowing about. I asked Heidi if I could see a picture of the worm. She said they didn't have their picture taken.

But even though I haven't seen a picture of Heidi's date, I think I could recognize him. Ever since Mike called him a worm, I've had a pretty good idea of what he looks like. Most of us have known a worm or two.

Now I'm not going to try to tell you how wonderful worms are. Maybe they *do* keep the air in the soil; maybe without them there would be no baby robins; maybe we need them to hook catfish. But unless we consult with some "worm-o-cologist," it's hard to come up with many attractive qualities for the basic earthworm.

Worms are slithery, little, skinny things, made of something that resembles purple Jello—and what's more, they eat dirt. A perfectly ordinary worm, six inches long, can thin himself to a foot-long slimy shoestring. Worms have no backbone, so you can wrap them around your finger—if you're weird enough to try.

In verse 6 of this psalm David compares himself to a worm: "I am a worm and not a man, scorned by men and despised by the people." The fact is, you've got to be pretty down and out to consider yourself a worm. If a kid came up to you and told you that he thinks he's a worm, you'd either feel sorry for him or tell him to grow up.

Yet great King David—the honored king and mighty warrior—tells God that he's a worm. And the reason he says it is clear. Without God's help and strength, David knows that he stands before men and women who hate him with no more power than nightcrawlers who lie in the wet grass before a couple of kids with flashlights. The nightcrawlers are powerless. They're beaten. All they can do is squirm for cover.

David doesn't want to be a nightcrawler. He wants God on his side.

But there's more to this psalm than David's pleading. Psalm 22 is full of pictures of Christ's own story: like Jesus Christ, David feels scorned and despised by people; he sees his oppressors cast lots for his clothing; he even asks God, as Christ did, why he has forsaken him. Some people call this psalm the "psalm of the cross."

That makes the business about being a worm even stranger. Think of Christ calling himself a worm—it would be almost a miracle in language. How could our Savior let himself be treated like a lousy worm?

The message of David's plea is that Christ suffered and died for us, became the butt of people's jokes, got himself kicked around for our sins, and died, shamefully, on the cross. Christ allowed himself to be treated like a worm and died for love. Incredible.

It's hard for us to think of ourselves as worms, Lord,
but what you did for us—giving your life so that we
may live, makes anything we do look pretty puny.
Thank you for loving us that much. Amen.

TRUST AND OBEY

....

Psalm 22:9-21

There's an old story about trust that's worth repeating.

A man is walking along a cliff somewhere, minding his own business, when all of a sudden something gives way beneath him. The man stumbles, slips, and falls over the edge. On his way down he manages to grab a rickety bush growing out of the rock. With both hands he hangs there, nothing beneath him but a couple hundred feet of jagged cliff—the kind of vista Wiley Coyote sees when the Roadrunner's got the best of him.

"Help!" he yells. "Someone please help!"

A voice comes out of nowhere. (Here's where the story gets a little corny, but stay with me.) "I'll help you," it says. "This is the Lord. I'll help you."

The man looks up and sees nothing, but he figures it's in the bag now. God is pulling for him.

"Do what I say," God commands.

Fair enough, the man figures. His alternative is a world-record trip down the mountain. "Okay, I'm with you," he says.

"Let go with your left hand," God says.

The hanging man debates with himself for a minute. He figures God will slip down a rope or a cable or call in an angelic helicopter. All right, the man figures, good enough. So he takes a good hold with his right hand and lets the left one go. "Okay, okay," he says, "now what?"

Then God says, "Let go with the other hand too."

A few seconds go by.

"Is there anybody else up there?" the man asks.

You've likely heard that one already, but it's one of those stories that's worth repeating because it so clearly describes *trust*—and *faith*, something Voltaire defines as "believing when it is beyond the power of reason to believe."

The poor joker hanging from the bush had no reason to believe he should let go. But trust and faith are sometimes beyond reason. Belief is sometimes irrational.

David claims in Psalm 22 that he has had faith (or trust in God) almost since the beginning of his life: "You brought me out of the womb; you made me trust in you even at my mother's breast." David is sure that God will be there again and again to help him.

The Bible says, "Faith is the substance of things hoped for, the evidence of things not seen." Now the fact of the matter is that faith is *not* something you can hold in your hands like a rope dropped from a helicopter. Faith has no substance. It can't be held or smelled, felt or weighed.

Yet the verse claims that faith—like trust in God—*is* substance, because faith is what makes hope real and touchable. It's the stuff from which invisible ropes are wound.

In this psalm David is surrounded by menacing bulls and lions. Furthermore, he claims he's no well-oiled Hulk Hogan: his bones are out of joint. He can't do it himself.

Yet he knows he will be delivered, even though he's got no reason to believe it. He's got faith—something invisible, but much better than a body slam.

....

Faith seems so slippery, Lord. It's not something we can hold on to. But let us keep it, even when the times get tough. Help us always—even at midnight—to trust you. Amen.

LEFT BEHIND

....

Psalm 22:9-31

Jerelyn Comisky is the oldest of the three daughters of Walter and Annjean Comisky, who recently separated. Jerelyn knew her parents' marriage was falling apart, but she still wasn't prepared for the split when it happened. The night her dad moved out, Jerelyn sat in the kitchen with both her sisters and wished she couldn't hear the words her mom and dad were screaming at each other just one thin wall away.

Paula, who's five, stopped eating her ice cream and held her hands over her ears. Ginger just cried.

Jerelyn started an extra job at a record store when it became clear to her that without her father's child-support (which he wasn't very faithful in supplying), her mother couldn't feed the family. Two jobs and school.

But the night that nearly killed Jerelyn was the night that she and Brad, a guy she goes with, saw her father at King Crab, sitting at an outdoor table along the ocean, having dinner and drinks with a girl wearing silver shoes. His shirt was unbuttoned almost down to his navel, and he wore three gold necklaces, like some Hollywood show-off.

Jerelyn told Brad to take her home immediately, and he did. In her room, she cried and tried to pray. But she couldn't. She had the feeling that there was nothing above her but ceiling lights and some wispy cobwebs nobody had time for now that her world had fallen completely apart.

"My God, my God, why have you forsaken me?" David asks.

There may well be times when we feel that God is ignoring us—that he's out somewhere watching neighborhood sparrows or counting the hairs that fall from some old man's head. Maybe he's distracted. Maybe there's a war someplace on the jungle coast of Outer Libitimi, and it takes everything he's got just to cover all the bloodshed and weeping.

When Jerelyn saw her father snapping crab legs and dipping them in little pots of butter with a woman young enough to be his daughter, she felt nauseous. She remembered what it was like to ride on his shoulders, to sit between his legs as he sprawled out on the floor in front of the TV. She'd seen him kiss her mother softly, watched them sway together in the kitchen, as if they both heard the same silent music.

Nothing meant so much to Jerelyn and her sisters as their parents. To see them broken, to see their family split, was to see the whole world crumble.

Jerelyn felt as if no one was protecting her. No one was watching out for her interests. No one loved her. No one cared, she thought.

She thought God had forgotten her. She needed him like she never had before, but he seemed to be out of earshot in some other world.

Does that happen to believers? Certainly.

Sometimes Christians feel forgotten. They feel as cast off as a child's teddy bear. Even David—the man God claimed was close to his own heart—felt he'd been stuck in a rat hole, a rotten corner where God's eyes never reached.

And even Christ himself, whose presence is in this psalm like an image just developing on a Polaroid snapshot, felt abandoned. Even Christ, in his dying hours, felt left behind.

But God is always there. Always. We're never left behind.

David knew it. And so does Jerelyn, really.

....

In the times we feel forgotten, Lord, always stay with us. Help us to lean on you all the time, and grant that we may always feel you near us. Amen.

DOMINION

....
Psalm 22:25-31

Around the time of the U.S. Civil War, Pietronella Baltus, an unmarried woman in her early thirties, lived on an estate just outside of Beesd, the Netherlands. She was a faithful believer, a Christian who read often about God and his world.

At the church where Miss Baltus worshiped, Rev. Kuyper, a young pastor just out of seminary, preached every Sunday. Pietronella Baltus didn't appreciate this young man's preaching. In fact, when she learned that Rev. Kuyper would be visiting her sometime just to talk, she told her friends she would have nothing to do with him. If he came to call, she would leave him standing out on her doorstep.

The young Rev. Kuyper, Pietronella Baltus explained, was not of the old school, or at least he wasn't of the same old school as she was. Back in seminary, Kuyper had stood and cheered when a popular professor named Scholten proclaimed publicly that he didn't believe Jesus had really risen—with his body—from death.

So Miss Baltus didn't think of the good Rev. Kuyper as a true believer. Not to believe Christ rose from the grave was not to believe in Christ, Miss Baltus thought, so she didn't have the time of day for the pastor.

Then someone reminded Pietronella Baltus that Kuyper had a soul just like everyone else—and that by not talking to him at all, she wasn't helping him. So this determined woman decided to talk to the young preacher. Maybe, she figured, she could teach him something.

Oddly enough, she did. This Rev. Kuyper—a man who could speak several languages fluently, who had read shelves full of important literature and won prizes for being a real brain—couldn't butt heads with little Pietronella Baltus. Her faith and conviction made such an impression on him that he began to believe she was right—that Christ really *did* arise and bring victory over death. Miss Bultus brought the young pastor to believe again.

From the little town of Beesd, Rev. Abraham Kuyper went on to become the leading theologian of his day and the Prime Minister of the Netherlands. He published a newspaper and wrote books read by thousands. Some people claim that few individuals were more important to European Christianity in the late nineteenth century than Abraham Kuyper.

In fact—even though I was born in the United States a quarter century after Kuyper died—he's shaped the way I think.

But what's most interesting about the story is that this little woman, a nobody from Beesd, changed the great Dr. Kuyper singlehandedly. Throughout his lifetime, he kept a picture of Pietronella Baltus on his desk to remind him of the importance of the plain and simple faith of plain and simple people.

Pietronella Baltus shows us clearly what David feels in verse 28: "dominion belongs to the Lord, and he rules over the nations." In God's hands, Pietronella Baltus became a powerhouse.

God rules. He determines who's big and who's small.

Abraham Kuyper became a great theologian, a powerful politician, and a prolific writer. But he wouldn't have done it without Pietronella Baltus—and God steering the world.

You are the Creator of the universe, the Lord of all of life. You know everything there is to know, including secrets about us that we aren't even aware of. And the best thing is that you are God. Thank you, Lord.
Amen.

THE WORLD'S GREATEST COKE

....
Psalm 23

Success is counted sweetest
By those who ne'er succeed.
To comprehend a nectar
Requirest sorest need.

Not one of all the purple host
Who took the flag today
Can tell the definition
So clear of victory

As he, defeated, dying,
On whose forbidden ear
The distant strains of triumph
Break, agonized and clear.

If you think some wounded soldier might have written this little poem, you're wrong. The author, Emily Dickinson, was a tiny lady who never married and rarely left home. She flitted, almost ghost-like, through her big, old house in Massachusetts.

The poem's idea appears in the first two lines: in any game, those who lose know best what it means to win. I know that sounds backwards, but try thinking it through: the absence of something good makes its presence even grander.

Try it this way. I remember the best Coke I ever drank. My wife and I were bumping along some dusty, desert roads out in the cotton fields around Chandler, Arizona, the sun curling up the upholstery in the empty school bus we were driving. We had no air conditioning, and we were out for more than an hour in the hottest air on earth. Finally we stopped at a hot dog stand and had a big Coke—so cold the ice made the glass slick. That day we could have made a commercial. It was the best Coke we'd ever had. Being without made being with much sweeter.

The last two verses of this poem make the same point with a war picture. No one knows victory, Dickinson says, like the man, defeated and dying, who hears his enemies cheer as they take the flag. Winners, she says, don't know the thrill of victory like those who've already suffered the agony of defeat.

Maybe the point is hard to understand here, but it's an important one—one that ties together Psalms 22 and 23. All that anguish that David (and Christ) felt in Psalm 22, all the talk about God forsaking them, all the complaints about bulls and lions and broken bones—all the hurt of Psalm 22 makes the peace and comfort of Psalm 23 even more lovely.

When we feel David's anxious fears in Psalm 22, we know that he knows what it feels like to be down and out. We know that he knows what it feels like to be away from God.

In Psalm 23 David's fears are calmed. He sits back on green grass, looks up at blue sky, and listens to the quiet flow of an old river. And he knows, better than those who've never lost, what victory in Christ's love is all about.

Knowing Psalm 22 makes Psalm 23 even more beautiful than it is by itself. It's a funny thing how that works, but it's often true. You've got to be without to know how good it is to be with.

David knows. He's been lost, but now he's found—and having been lost has made being found incredibly good.

Even better—so much better—than the world's greatest Coke.

....

Lord, thank you for guiding our lives. We know that you have promised that all things work together for good for those who love you. Thank you for making us feel the comfort of your love. Amen.

NO WANTING

....
Psalm 23:1-3

When Donald Trump is at home in New York, he sometimes flies around in his ten-million dollar helicopter, a ten-seat French Puma he claims is the safest in the world.

His cottage on the ocean at Palm Beach, Florida, has 118 rooms, its own private golf course, and over four hundred feet of beach. But for quick weekend getaways, he and his wife prefer their Greenwich, Connecticut, hideaway, a modest 47-room bungalow they picked up for a song at only two million.

What's Trump worth? Some say as much as three billion dollars. In addition to operating all kinds of casinos in Las Vegas and Atlantic City, he owns some of New York City's finest real estate, an airline company, his own Boeing 727, and a half dozen helicopters. Not bad for a guy just over forty years old.

Perhaps the gem, however, is the twenty-nine million dollar yacht named, appropriately, the *Trump Princess,* a cute little runabout with gold-plated shower nozzles, a rotating sun bed and, of all things, an inside waterfall.

Trump's New York penthouse takes up all kinds of space in his own Trump Tower. It's a homey little nook with an eighty-foot living room that Trump has outfitted with onyx baseboards. And guess what else it has? You knew already? Another waterfall.

Trump, who says, "It's all a game really," plays well and hard at the Monopoly board he's set up over New York's fanciest avenues. When anyone gets in his way or tries to fight him, he calls in his palace guard—ten different legal firms that take care of his affairs.

What's more, he likes fights. "I love to have enemies," he says. "I like beating my enemies to the ground."

Nice guy, too, besides having all those bucks.

"The Lord is my shepherd," David says. "I shall not be in want." Neither will Donald Trump. Not on earth, anyway.

He's become a symbol of the lust for wealth that haunts the dreams of so many today—people who want to be the high rollers, the ones who make big bucks. With all that loot, Trump shall not want; if he does, he'll just buy. He knows there are just two ways to live in this world. One is with God. The other is with big bucks. He's taken the second option, and he's trumped just about everyone in the game.

"Hey, life is life," he says. "We're here for a short time. When we're gone, most people don't care, and in some cases they're quite happy about it."

If that's what he believes, then what he does makes great sense. If all there is to life is one big swing through, one chance to let loose, then you may as well push the pedal to the floor and get what you can, because you only go around once.

The other way to live is by faith and praise, by trusting that God is the Creator and Governor of the whole world, and by praising that very God for loving us so much that he sent his Son to die for us—a free gift of love, no additional payments.

With that gift, we will never want—not even when Trump will.

Because someday he will. Count on it.

That fact you can take to the bank.

We confess that there are lots of things in the world that we'd love to have. Help us always to see that nothing we own ever gives us the love and peace that your love promises. In Jesus' name, Amen.

RALPH'S RESTORATION

....
Psalm 23:1-4

Ralph Eliot figured he *had* to swing the big deal with the Masters Corporation, because if he didn't—well, he just didn't want to think about it.

He checked over the blueprints once again, figured in the extra duct work the project would need, tried to estimate the labor costs, and penciled in what kind of money it would take for the masonry. Three times he ran all the numbers through the calculator to be sure he had the figures down.

It was four o'clock, and the bid had to be in by five. He stared down at the coffee on his desk, the fourth cup he'd had since early afternoon—and he'd told himself he had to cut down.

His son Josh had a ball game in fifteen minutes that Ralph had promised he'd be at, but he just didn't feel right about the totals, not without taking one last look at the place where the new complex was going up. Maybe there was something out there that he hadn't seen. He figured he'd have enough time to take one last swing past the place. He'd apologize to Josh later.

Ralph grabbed the file, ran out to the car, and jumped in. He jammed the stick into reverse and started to back out. Brakes screamed, and he stopped on a dime. Right behind him a guy in a shop truck stared angrily. Ralph hadn't even looked.

He felt his heart racing. He and his wife were celebrating their anniversary tomorrow, and he'd planned on stopping somewhere to order flowers. He would still get that in somehow, he told himself. And the meeting tonight—school board. He hadn't looked over the agenda, and he knew he was supposed to make a recommendation about repaving the parking lot.

The whole world was racing, he thought. When he came to the red light at the end of Springer Avenue, he swung into the right lane to save time and turned quickly. A woman in a station wagon tried to swerve to avoid him, but she pounded into his left back fender, flipping Ralph's Toyota, and pushing him into a utility pole.

Ralph Eliot sustained a concussion that afternoon and forgot everything: the estimates, the ball game, the flowers, and the parking lot recommendation. His mind was wiped clean.

Was it God who caused the accident? No. It was Ralph. He didn't look closely when he turned.

But does that mean that God had nothing to do with it? Probably not. One of the interesting words in Psalm 23 is the second word of the second verse: "He *makes* me lie down in green pastures. . . ." Sometimes we don't want to lie down. We live as if life is Disneyland and we've only got one hour.

Sometimes God stops us in our tracks to remind us that the hustle and bustle of life is only one part of being a Christian. The other part is thinking, meditation—something we might call contemplation. The second part doesn't make us any money, but it's important.

In Psalm 90, Moses asks the Lord, "Teach us to number our days aright, that we may gain a heart of wisdom." Wisdom one finds in green pastures.

Ralph would have liked the idea of slowing down, but that doesn't mean he'd have done it. Sometimes God makes us lie down in green pastures, leads us beside quiet waters, and restores our souls.

He knows our best interests.

We don't know why some things happen, Lord, but we know that you control our lives. Thank you for being our God, our Father, and our friend. Amen.

A WALK WITH THE SHEPHERD

....
Psalm 23:4-6

Arnold Fessington rolled up his sleeves and sat in the chair where he sat every week. He was so close to Bill—right across the table—yet so far away from the freedom Bill had, freedom to come and go.

"You want me to read anything special, Arn?" Bill asked.

"Don't even read it," Arnie said. "Just speak it to me again. Recite it. Do the shepherd psalm, will you—like you do?"

So Bill spoke it, from memory, all the way through.

"When you say it like that," Arnie said, "I feel like something in me busted right through the bars. 'And I shall dwell in the house of the Lord forever.' " Arnie laughed out loud.

"You're free," Bill said. "You know that, don't you?"

"I know it," Arnie said. "Lord God Almighty, I know it."

* * * * * *

Andy's mom said Grandma wouldn't live till his graduation, so whenever he took his turn sitting beside her, he thought it might be his last. He didn't want to lose her.

Grandma pointed at the Bible beneath the light beside the bed, and Andy took it in both hands. He wished he were a preacher so he would know what passage would be just perfect now.

She nodded at him—her thin hair lying beneath her head like a kerchief of gray silk—her way of telling him to read.

He put the Bible down and let it fall open to Psalm 23. She'd heard it so often, he didn't think she would hear a word he said. It was such an old passage, one everybody knew.

But he read it, and when he finished she smiled—not at him but up, at the ceiling, like a kid who's discovered a new idea.

* * * * * *

Marie couldn't even guess how many guys had died attempting the invasion. They'd started that morning with so much enthusiasm about taking Europe back from Hitler. She'd seen them at the base, proud and anxious, but afraid of the bunkers on Normandy.

The ward was quiet except for the occasional moans from some whose pain she couldn't stop. For a minute at least, she could rest. Then more would come. The flow would go on for days. Her hands shook from long hours of repairing broken bodies and comforting boys tortured by the thought of facing life without arms or legs.

Marie had no Bible, so she sat there at the desk, closed her eyes, and slowly repeated the twenty-third Psalm quietly, only to herself. Peace ran like new blood into her wrists. God would be with her. His rod and staff would comfort her—and them.

* * * * * *

After eleven, the house was deadly silent. Jerelyn's little sisters were already asleep. She'd done the laundry, cleaned up the kitchen, even scrubbed the back hall. Her mom was at work. Jerelyn hadn't seen her father since the night at the restaurant.

She hadn't found time to study for the biology test she had to take tomorrow. There was too much work to do at home. Now it was almost midnight, and she still had to get her sisters' clothes ready for school in the morning. She wouldn't do as well on the test as she wanted, but tonight her mind couldn't hack cell morphology.

A half hour later as she got ready for bed, Jerelyn felt like crying, so she did. But as she wept, she picked up her Bible and turned to Psalm 23. She read it slowly, again and again and again, until, exhausted, she laid down the book beside her and slept, the bed lamp still burning in the silent darkness.

Thank you, Lord, for gifts like Psalm 23, little passages of Scripture that we can carry weightlessly throughout our lives. Thank you for the peace of this psalm. Amen.

HONESTY II

When Matt looked at the Mama's Boys tapes stacked on his dresser, he nearly got sick. He wished he'd never seen them before, even though a hundred other guys from school would have taken them and never felt a thing, especially if they'd gotten them from Whitney. She could have any guy she wanted.

But something in those tapes didn't sit right. So when he got into bed that night, Matt stuck Amy Grant in his deck—even though he hadn't listened to her since he was a kid.

When he was a boy, Matt's parents had always kissed him goodnight and asked him to say a prayer. But that had stopped somewhere around the fourth grade or so. And when they stopped coming up with him, he pretty much stopped chugging through the little prayer he had always said—"Now I lay me. . . ." Sometimes his dad or mom would still ask him if he'd said his prayers, and he'd usually say he did, even when he didn't.

Maybe it was Adkins—what he'd said about being honest to God— that made Matt think of praying tonight. Maybe Adkins made him do it, and maybe it had something to do with listening to Amy Grant instead of the Mama's Boys.

Matt was almost positive Whitney had lifted those tapes. Three of them times what? Eight bucks a piece or so? Almost twenty-five bucks.

Maybe he was wrong, of course. How on earth could a skinny kid like Whitney get out of Music Unlimited tucking three of those long plastic tape holders under her jean jacket? She'd look like she was hiding a swing set. Maybe she didn't steal them.

Matt flipped out the light and looked over at the stack on his dresser. The tapes seemed to glow as if they were radioactive.

"I've got to give them back," he told himself. "I'll just tell her that I dubbed them and that now she can have them back." That way he wouldn't have to worry about where they came from, wouldn't have to accuse her of something that might make her angry. That way, he thought, I can wash my hands of the whole deal.

There they lay, glowing.

But he knew it was deeper than just the tapes. There was something about Whitney that he liked, and it wasn't just the fact that every other guy in school thought she was great. There was something about her . . . .

Maybe Adkins was right, he thought. Maybe he ought to pray, even if he didn't know what to ask. So he did.

Matt stretched back and closed his eyes, his hands up over his head, folded, the way he used to fold them when he was a kid. He told God about the tapes, about Whitney and what he figured she was up to. And he told God about what he thought of Whitney, how she was better than just a sleazeball who stole tapes.

"I don't have anything to ask really—" he said, "—maybe that you help me through this somehow, whatever it is." When the words didn't come, Matt felt like a car running out of gas. "Maybe that you help me do the right thing—maybe that's what I'm asking for," he said, "because I don't know what I'm doing."

Matt opened his eyes in the darkness, and the ceiling seemed one hundred feet high. Beside him, the tapes still glowed on the dresser.

He lay there thinking that maybe something like electricity was going to surge through him all of a sudden, light him up; or that maybe God would write a message over the walls, spell something up on the ceiling, like one of those airplanes selling suntan lotion on a long poster flung out behind its tail.

But nothing happened, nothing like that anyway.

"It seems to me this isn't the right way to pray, just to talk like this," he said, "but Adkins says to tell you everything. What do I have to tell you for anyway, if you know already? Shoot, you run everything."

He stopped suddenly, because he realized that he'd never before joshed with the Lord God Almighty as if he were just some guy right there in the room.

"It's these tapes that are causing all the trouble," he said. "Why don't you just put them back where they came from?"

That was a dumb thing to say, he thought.

"You can do anything, can't you?" he said. "Anything at all. Anything you want to do." It was an amazing thought. "If that's true, then why don't you help me?" It didn't seem like such a big thing to ask. "Help me get out of this."

He didn't know what to say anymore, so he threw in the last words like he thought he was supposed to. "Amen," he said, "that's all there is tonight."

A few minutes later Matt heard footsteps on the stairs. His parents were coming to bed. He heard his father pass the bathroom and his sister's room, then stop at his. The door swung open, creaking.

"Goodnight, Matt," his father said. "You pray?"

"Sure," Matt said. "Just finished now."

When no one else listens, Lord, we know you will.
Give us the ability and the desire to tell you what's
on our minds, to be open with you, our Friend and
Savior. Amen.

WHO, ME?

....

Psalm 38

Last January an ice storm turned our whole town into a skating rink, including the sidewalk that slopes down from my back door. The only way to manage it, I found, was by taking a running slide, my hands stuck out at my sides for balance.

Thursday the sun came out. The temperature never notched a degree above freezing, but bald spots emerged where the ice was thinnest. I'm forty-one years old, and I weigh two hundred and too-much. Maybe I'm nuts, too, but when I left the house that Thursday, I never thought about a thaw.

I skipped out the back door, put both feet down on the ice, and skated down the sidewalk in my size fourteens. I never even saw the bare cement. When I hit it, I pitched forward, almost out of control, and tried to hit the brakes. But when I jammed my feet beneath me, they hit pure ice and took off toward the sky.

I looked, just for a second, like a varsity cheerleader in a rousing toe-touch. There I was, staring at my shoes, poised for a perfect one-point landing, all two-hundred plus pounds suspended in mid-air before a shock I feared would register 4.5 on the Richter scale somewhere near Santa Clara, a couple thousand miles away.

I hit with the kind of force that makes children scream. I landed on the flat of my back, cracked a rib, knocked myself completely out of wind, and smashed back muscles I didn't know I had.

Pain ripped through my back and shoulders, wound itself around my chest like a steel band, and completely shut off my air; but all I thought about, from the moment I smacked down until I could raise my head and look around, was whether anyone saw my spastic gymnastic stunt.

I saw a car pass, a gold Ford. When I see the driver yet today, I wonder whether she caught my act.

Humiliation, like guilt, is something we all take great pains to avoid. If you've ever been caught red-handed at something you shouldn't have done, you know how well your instincts for self-preservation really operate. "Who, me?"

Nobody likes being caught. Most everyone I know will do anything to avoid blame or humiliation. "The devil made me do it," TV comedian Flip Wilson used to say, and everyone laughed.

Psalm 38 is a psalm about falling—not on ice, but into sin. In this psalm David confesses that he's earned God's anger. He's not trying to hide, not blaming anybody else. "My wounds fester and are loathsome because of my sinful folly," he says.

Admitting guilt is terribly difficult. It takes a strong person to admit weakness.

David's first step back to God's love is simply confessing. "He's half-absolved that has confessed," wrote Matthew Prior.

That's the strength of Psalm 38—strength in weakness.

When we're guilty, Lord, we usually try to get out of it in any way we can. Nobody wants to be wrong, and nobody wants to get caught. But you know it all. You know how cheap our pride really is. Forgive us— in the name of your Son, Amen.

SHIMMERING HELLFIRE

If you want to hear hellfire and brimstone, listen to this sermon:

> The God that holds you over the pit of hell, much as one
> holds a spider or some loathsome insect over the fire, ab-
> hors you, and is dreadfully provoked: his wrath towards you
> burns like fire; he looks upon you as worthy of nothing else,
> but to be cast into the fire; he is of purer eyes than to bear
> to have you in his sight; you are ten thousand times more
> abominable in his eyes than the most hateful and
> venomous serpent is in ours. You have offended him in-
> finitely more than ever a stubborn rebel did his prince; and
> yet it is nothing but his hand that holds you from falling into
> the fire every moment. It is to be ascribed to nothing else,
> that you did not go to hell the last night; that you were suf-
> fered to awake again in this world after you closed your
> eyes to sleep. And there is no other reason to be given why
> you have not dropped into hell since you arose in the morn-
> ing, but that God's hand has held you up. There is no other
> reason to be given why you have not gone to hell since you
> have sat here in the house of God, provoking his pure eyes
> by your sinful wicked manner of attending his solemn wor-
> ship. Yea, there is nothing else that is to be given as a
> reason why you do not this very moment drop down into
> hell.

Ouch!

With that sermon, Jonathan Edwards, a seventeenth-century
preacher, probably could have made the *Guinness Book of World
Records* for references to hell in one paragraph. If you sat through a
sermon like that today, you'd likely feel the pew begin to burn beneath
you.

Chances are, my grandfather was raised with a picture of God much closer to Edwards's—an angry, snarling God dangling humanity over an inferno by the thinnest of threads—than I was.

What's more, I think my children's picture of God might be completely different than either mine or my grandfather's. They think of God as a sweet old man in a rocking chair who gives quarters to kids who come around and sit in his lap—something like a shopping-mall Santa Claus.

Who is right? Both, probably. God loves us. He gave his own Son to die for our sins, after all. Who could do more?

But maybe my kids ought to see this other picture—the snarling God Edwards paints and the God David describes in Psalm 38. "Go ahead and discipline me," David says, "but cool off some before you do." Does God spit and fume? David says he does.

What's more, David claims that God's own arrows create the pain he's feeling: "For *your* arrows have pierced me," he says in verse 2, "and *your* hand has come down upon me." The God David is talking to here is no pot-bellied Santa Claus.

Does God shoot his people? No, he loves them. But he does rage against their sins.

The fact is, David says, God gets angry—very angry.

But even when God is angry, David doesn't turn away from him. David knows that this angry God of fire and brimstone is still the God who loves him. He is still the God in whom David finds forgiveness and new strength—the God who keeps his promises.

And he's made the same promises to us.

Maybe it's too easy not to be afraid of you today,
Lord. If we don't know your power, we don't respect
you as God of our universe. We're sorry for making
you trivial sometimes. We know you're not. You're
our God. Amen.

SUPERMAN CRIPPLED

....
Psalm 38:5-12

One of the great photos of the 1988 Olympics was of the finish of the one-hundred-meter dash. Carl Lewis, who'd already won a couple of medals, couldn't catch Ben Johnson, Canada's great hope to become "the world's fastest human."

When Johnson finished, his bulky arms raised above his head in victory, his wide smile made the world proud to have witnessed not only a great victory, but a new world's record at the world's premier track meet.

But everyone knows the rest of the story. Not long after that race, Johnson was stripped of his medal—and the title—for using steroids to pork up his bulk. What had been a victory romp around the track was really a long, galloping lie. Pumped up on steroids, Johnson was more than the sum of his parts.

When accused, he lied again, just as he had when he posed as a winner during his victory lap. Johnson the victor was really Johnson the loser.

Johnson says now that one of the first things he did when he came back to Toronto was walk into his room and pick up the bottle of steroids he'd been using. He says he turned it in his hands and whipped it up against the wall, where it smashed, like his dreams.

The world's fastest human, a man blessed by God Almighty with a body worthy of a myth—forearms and biceps thick as bridge cables, thighs round as trees, calves perfectly shaped above the thinnest of ankles—the man with a perfect body became a Cain, marked for life with deceit, a man whose word would never again be fully trusted.

"Yes . . . I lied," the Jamaican immigrant claimed in his final day of testimony to a Canadian drug commission. "I was ashamed for my family. My friends . . . young people looked up to me, and I was a mess."

That brokenness from the man with the perfect body.

"I want to tell them to be honest," he told the commission, when asked what he wanted to say to young people. "Don't take drugs. I've been there. I know what it's like to cheat."

Everyone knows the hazards of steroid use today. Scientists have linked them with heart disease, liver trouble, problems with the urinary tract, and even skin diseases.

But even if Ben Johnson never suffers from the problems steroids can create, he is already scarred. He's broken the public trust. He's lied. He's been found a sham. It's not the steroids that make him depressed today; it's the lying and the guilt.

Ben Johnson discovered something that David learned centuries ago—that sins of the flesh, of the body, sometimes only reflect the sins of the spirit. "My back is filled with searing pain; there is no health in my body. I am feeble and utterly crushed; I groan in anguish of heart." Anguish of heart—that's a disease that won't show up on a hospital monitor.

Ben Johnson's incredible body pushed him through the tape in the greatest footrace in the world. But his heart failed him.

To see him today is to see a man, like David, "bowed down and brought low." But also, like David, not without hope.

Forgive our sins, God. We know that when we don't stand clean before you, the whole world can look feeble and sick. We don't feel like being alive. Clean us. Make us strong. Amen.

FALLEN SAINTS

....
Psalm 38:12-22

The town where I grew up, a little Wisconsin town named Oostburg, prided itself on its strict cleanliness and its churches. Because of our religious beliefs about the Sabbath, no one in Oostburg washed their cars on Sunday or mowed their lawns. At our annual Fourth of July picnic, no one sold beer.

Some towns around us thought Oostburg people acted like they were better than the rest, maybe a tad more holy. So people from these towns enjoyed catching people from Oostburg doing something wrong—getting drunk or something. It made saints human.

When I was a teenager, I worked at a state park on Lake Michigan, a place where families came to camp. Sometimes kids came down to camp all by themselves to get away from their parents' eyes.

At night, the campground could get a little rowdy with those kids around, unsupervised. So it was the duty of the guys who worked nights to know the sites where kids were staying, just to keep an eye out for trouble.

Some guys I worked with used to watch the kids from Oostburg closer than anybody else. "There are Oostburg kids in site 23," one of them would say. "Nail them if you can."

When they said things like that, it made me angry—even though they probably didn't remember I was one of those Oostburg kids. I didn't think it was right for them to treat the kids from my hometown as if they were a special breed.

But I understand why they did it.

My college roommate didn't believe that movies were good for his spiritual health. One night we hog-tied him into going. We paid his ticket, bought him popcorn, and offered him a free meal just to get him into a theater. When he came out, we asked him what he thought. The movie was no skin flick, but he told us flat out that he was never going again.

Even so, it was fun to bring a saint down.

Few things seem to fascinate people more than fallen saints. In the last year I must have seen the picture of Jimmy Swaggart crying before his congregation a dozen times. And few *Nightline* programs scored as well with American audiences as those programs in which Ted Koppel interviewed Jim and Tammy Bakker, the other fallen TV evangelists.

David understood that fascination. He knew that people take great joy in seeing the righteous dirtied up. He understood that his problems—and he had them, after all—made his enemies uproariously happy. That's why he asked the Lord (v.16) not to let them gloat or exalt when his feet slipped.

But you can bet they did. "King seduces woman after seeing her in bathtub—Has husband killed." What a headline. Picking off fallen saints is simply great sport.

Remember Samson? On the biggest night of his life, on the night he brought down the temple to a heap of rubble and death, he was the sport of the Philistines. "Bring on Samson to entertain us. You know— the blind guy, the body-builder who fell to our sweetheart, Delilah. Ha ha! Where is the clown?"

But when saints fall, the real tragedy is not reputation or pride. David understood that when he was the butt of unbelievers' jokes, God himself took some licks.

And that made David's pain even greater.

··

God, our Father, when we're laughed at for what we believe, you are laughed at too. Keep us from falling, but punish those who laugh at you through us, your children. Amen.

PSALM 38

HONESTY III

At school the next day, Matt tried to stay away from Whitney. But he knew she could tell he was avoiding her and that sooner or later she'd come after him. She was like that.

"You stuck up, or what?" she said when she found him on his paper route. "You didn't say one word to me today."

He flipped off his overhead bag and stuck the last twenty papers in the front basket of his bike. "What do you mean?" he asked.

"I mean, like you're avoiding me. I can tell."

He slapped down the kickstand with his foot and grabbed a paper. "I got to do this," he said, walking away. "Sorry."

"I mean at school, Matt," she said, "all day."

He rolled up the paper as he walked up Ivy's front sidewalk. The door was open, and he heard the sound of cartoons drifting out from the family room. Sometimes he wished he were still a kid.

He jammed the paper in the mail slot and turned around. Whitney was balancing on her bike, toes down on the ground on both sides, her long arms stretched down to the handlebars.

"Even Amy noticed it," she told him. "She says, 'What's Matt mad about?' And I'm going, 'I wish I knew'—really."

He had to talk to her. "There's nothing wrong," he said, shrugging his shoulders. "I just didn't have anything to say."

"You're mad," she said. "I know you are, Matt."

"I'm not mad," he told her. "Stop saying that."

"You are too."

He got back on his bike and pedaled down the sidewalk, Whitney right behind him. If he only knew the right words so he wouldn't hurt her—but he couldn't find the way to say it. "You stealing, Whitney?"— that's what came to his mind. But that wasn't any good. He had to be soft.

"I didn't make the Pom line," she said when he stopped at Whisnant's. "Stupid drills anyway, parading around out there."

He'd forgotten about the big tryouts. She'd wanted to make it—really bad. It was all she had talked about for weeks.

"Did you hear me?" she said.

He grabbed another paper, starting to roll it in his hands. "Who did?" he asked.

"Amy, Sherry, Candy Wolf, Diane, Lisa Carlson—almost all of my friends—"

"That's too bad," he said, looking at her for the first time. "This way at least you don't have to wear those silly outfits."

"They're getting new ones," she told him. "Miss Fredricks said she'd let the squad pick them out."

Matt flipped the paper backhand, and it landed on the porch.

"Aren't you going to say anything?" she said.

He turned around to face her. "You feel bad?" he asked.

She turned away.

"I'm sorry," he said.

"I was counting on it," she told him, "too much I guess. I mean, I'm no hotshot or anything, but I just figured I was popular enough, you know—"

"You are."

"Not popular *enough*, I guess."

He felt sorry for her. He really did.

"By the way, I've got something for you," she said.

He swung his leg over the bike and waited. She reached in her bag and pulled out two tapes. "Check this out," she said, handing them over. "*Brass Thistles—Greatest Hits.* You love them."

He didn't take the tapes right away, but she pushed them at him.

"Take 'em," she said. "They're my brother's, and he never listens to them anymore—"

"I'll make copies," Matt said.

"Just keep 'em," she said. "Nobody'll know the difference."

A week ago he and Whitney had been standing at a bin in the mall, and he'd held onto the Brass Thistles for ten minutes—long enough to figure out how many papers he'd have to peddle to pay for it.

He had to say it now, find some words to get it out. "This is almost twenty bucks," he said. "I can't just keep them."

"They're for you," she said. "Can't I give you a present if I want to? It's a free country."

He took the tapes from her.

"My mom's going to be really disappointed," she told him. "She was sure I'd make Pom. I'm going to have to tell her now." She shook her head slowly, and her eyes fell to the sidewalk.

This wasn't the right time, he told himself. He'd do it sometime, but not now. She already felt bad, and he couldn't bring it up—not this afternoon—so he slipped Brass Thistles into the bag of papers.

He felt those Thistles tapes burning what papers he had left.

"How'd you do on math?" he asked, as the two of them pedaled toward Maple Drive.

Sometimes we give in way too easily, Lord. We lack the strength to fight for what we know is right. We want to be accepted and liked. We don't want to lose friends. Give us strength to face pressure. In Jesus' name, Amen.

THE WONDER OF THE HEAVENS

....

Psalm 104:1-9

When I was a boy, I remember staring down into a perfectly blue in-land lake that people claimed was "bottomless." It couldn't have been, of course, but to me the idea was spooky. If I could get myself into one of those steel diving suits and sink down, down, down, who knows where I'd come out? Besides, anything bottomless had to be stocked with dark and horrifying creatures in a dim, nightmarish world.

"Nessie," Scotland's lovable dinosaur-like monster, supposedly sur-faces once in awhile in Loch Ness, another body of water people claim is bottomless. I don't know if Nessie really exists, but if she does, it's only right that she shows her face in a lake that "has no bottom."

We can't quite understand what we can't really imagine. All we do is roll our eyes and shudder. Infinity, foreverness—a bottomless lake. That stuff seems terribly mysterious.

God, of course, is infinite—beyond time and space. We can't say that God is spending the night in Los Angeles tonight or that he grew up in the Middle East. God is everywhere, and no matter how hard we try, we can't even sketch his silhouette.

What the psalmist knows, however, is that maybe we *can* glimpse something of God's presence if we look closely at the world he's created. Psalm 104 brings praise to God by describing the works of his hands. It starts by looking at the heavens—light itself, the sky, clouds, and wind.

The sky is maybe the biggest thing anyone can ever really see. Yet the psalmist says that God wraps himself in light (wow!) as if it were a car blanket, uses the sky for a pup tent, and rides the wind from his driver's seat in the clouds. God's infinity outruns our longest yardstick, but maybe the sky hints at how big he really is.

Unless you live in the country, you've probably not looked up at a sky full of stars recently. City lights normally blind us from seeing what's up there in the darkness. But if you take the time to look up at the heavens some night, you'll see what the psalmist saw and felt in an infinity of stars.

For hundreds of years people have watched the skies to figure out where they are, to determine the time, or to get a weather forecast. My father spent World War II in the South Pacific. He used to pull this little ditty on me sometimes. "Red in the morning," he'd say, "sailor takes warning. Red at night—sailor's delight." Most often, he was right.

But the psalmist isn't looking at the skies to determine the weather. He wants to get a picture of God the creator, and he starts, in Psalm 104, with the sky.

There's an old story I like about the French Revolution. It goes like this: A young hotdog revolutionary told an old peasant how faith in God was going to be a thing of the past once the revolution took over. "I will have your steeples torn down," he snarled, "so that all the memories of your old superstitions will be gone."

The old man smiled. "You can't pull down the stars," he said.

The heavens declare the glory of God. Isn't he a wonder?

Dear Lord, we know we will never understand you. We can't, because you're the Lord of all. You know all of us at every moment. You're everywhere. And you love us. Thank you. In Jesus' name, Amen.

JUST SAY THE WORD

....
Psalm 104:10-25

The massive volcano that almost destroyed Washington's Mount St. Helens on May 18, 1980, came as no real surprise. The nearly perfect mountain seemed edgy for months, even years. Geologists had long before predicted that sometime before the year 2000, the almost ten-thousand-foot-high mountain would blow its lid as no other mountain in North America had done for centuries.

What was surprising was the titanic power of the blast. What began in a series of strong earthquakes two months before ended at 8:32 on a Sunday morning in May, when thirteen hundred square feet of the mountain's north face disappeared in a blast that was five hundred times more powerful than the explosion created by the atomic bomb dropped on Hiroshima. Chunks of stone twelve feet in diameter rocketed from the volcano, and temperatures reached two thousand degrees Fahrenheit in the scorching flow of lava that spewed from the gaping hole in the mountain. A ten-ton Caterpillar parked ten miles from the blast was blown a thousand feet through the air.

Volcanic ash blew as high as ninety thousand feet up before spreading out in the high winds and sweeping across half the continent in a real cloud of dust. Closer to the mountain, the ash fell like a quilt of smudge, sometimes up to eight inches deep, on towns and cities and farmland.

What was left on the mountain was a muddy mound fifteen miles long that turned a beautiful river valley into muck and sludge, poked full of dead timber. More than a hundred fifty square miles of fir and spruce and alpine lakes were completely destroyed by the horizontal blast that reshaped the entire mountain.

Seventy people were killed or presumed dead after that explosion. Countless deer, elk, bears, mountain lions, and other animals were also destroyed. Sixty thousand acres of federal wildlife habitat were scorched or severely damaged by the destruction of vegetation.

And those were only the immediate losses. The effects of Mount St. Helens's wrath were seen for years afterward: tons of debris had to be cleaned up, mountains of ash needed hauling, and clogged-up sewage-treatment plants throughout the region required millions of dollars of work.

In addition, the whole region's potential for attracting tourists declined as woodlands turned into spooky, moon-like landscapes. The government had to spend hundreds of millions of dollars repairing shipping channels in the Columbia and Cowlitz Rivers and replacing bridges and highways destroyed by mud slides.

The Mount St. Helens volcano caused monumental destruction. What incredible power!

But wait just a minute. We're talking about destructive power here—what about creative power?

God destroyed that mountain. But he made it first, and it didn't take him any time at all. The Bible says all he did is say the word, and Mount St. Helens was. Didn't cost him a thing.

What's more, he made the whole Cascade mountain range at the very same instant. In fact, throw in Kilimanjaro, Vesuvius, Pike's Peak, and all of Hawaii's finest. God made them all, put all the ranges together—poof!—with just one word.

You want power? Consider creation.

You made this whole world out of nothing, Lord. It's hard for us to imagine what that must have been like as you formed the oceans and the continents. But we know you did it. And we know that this world is yours—and so are we. Thank you for your Son.
Amen.

CARTOONS

....

Psalm 104:19-35

It takes a heart of nails not to wince when Bambi's mother dies. One horrifying shot rings through the forest, and suddenly this darling fawn is a motherless beggar on the paths of the woods. In Walt Disney's famous cartoon, of course, all the wilderness creatures help out—squirrels, rabbits, even owls—and a life begun in sadness ends in joy. Ah, Disney! What a world.

It's not hard to make nature into a cartoon. Almost any writer can do it. How about this: "A robe of morning dew sparkles in dawn's burnished light, making the meadow a queen."

Or another: "The ageless pines lose their color at night, but the moon scatters the forest's darkness, splinters the night with long, rectangular shafts."

As long as I'm in the mood, let's try just one more: "Its first bath over, the new-born calf stiffens each wobbly leg beneath him, one at a time, then stands slowly for its first round of applause from an eager, waiting world."

Charming, don't you think? Cute.

And real too.

But each of those little, sweetheart sentences is only part of the truth. If you've ever watched a farmer help a cow give birth, what you've seen isn't particularly pretty. If you've ever walked through an acre of wet grass in the morning, you know that although it may look pretty, you end up cold and wet, your pants and shoes heavy as mud. Things aren't always as adorable as they seem in cartoons.

Psalm 104, a poet's view of creation, doesn't make God's world into a cartoon. There's some Bambi stuff in here—whales frolicking in the ocean, the stork at home in the pines, wild donkeys quenching their thirst in a perfect meadow pond. But, the psalmist says, when night falls, the beasts of the forest prowl.

Some people, by instinct, hate cats. I'm not one of them. Our cat, like yours maybe, has a dozen names, none of them in any book. We call her Doots and Woo and Terwee and an assortment of other silly baby-talk handles that we use because our pet can be such a dear.

But if you've ever watched a cat kill a mouse, you've seen bloody treachery. Somewhere buried in layers of instinct lies the cat's own brand of torture: making the mouse suffer as deliciously long as possible before the slaughter. Who knows where a house cat ever learned such horror, but they all know it—and practice it.

The world we live in is no cartoon. Perhaps that's why my favorite verses of Psalm 104 are not the ones about the beauties of the mountains or the seas. My favorites are verses 27-29. Read them again. You, Lord God, are in control here, even of the animal's terror, the psalmist says: *you* open your hand; *you* hide your face; *you* take away their breath; *you* send your spirit.

God reigns, and that's the beauty of the forest.

*You ride in every storm, Lord. You walk through
every forest and watch the plains like a landowner.
The world belongs to you—every inch of it. We
praise you, our God and Creator. Amen.*

BAD ENDINGS

....

Psalm 104:31-35

Pardon me for saying this, but I'm not in love with the last verse of Psalm 104. Of course it's wonderful that the psalmist concludes with a pair of chest-thumping praises to God. What gets me is what he says before that: "may sinners vanish from the earth and the wicked be no more."

Sometimes I'm surprised and a little put off by the unbelievably bloody things some of the psalm writers asked for. For instance, in Psalm 137 (we'll take a closer look at that one later) the writer asks God to take the children of his enemies and bash their heads against stones. Isn't that going a little far?

What the psalmist says in the last verse of this chapter isn't that wretchedly violent, of course, but it seems to me that this perfectly beautiful psalm about creation is marred by the wish that sinners would vanish. I mean, doesn't the writer consider himself a sinner? Let him who is without sin take the first potshot. What's that silly reference to sinners got to do with "all things bright and beautiful"?

Imagine for a minute that we *could* wish some really serious sinners dead. Who would we include in a bundle of sinners suitable for burning?

We could take the drug dealers, the slime of society, and throw in a couple hundred pornography merchants, just to get a good fire going. Add a score of devil worshipers and every death-row convict now awaiting execution. Throw in child-killers, Adolph Hitler and his cohorts, abortionists, spouse-beaters, those who prey on the elderly, casino owners, beer distributors, trash-movie makers, rapists, a dozen or so rotten novelists, TV evangelists who go out on their wives, women who abandon their children—or abort them, and add the town drunk (there's still more room).

Well hold on, you're probably saying. We're going to ask God to rain down a firestorm and incinerate all of those people?

I know a man in our church who beat his wife, and a kid down the block got thrown in a detention center for selling dope. I'm not so sure that *all* these folks have to go.

That's the point. In the world we live in today, it's not easy to target who is headed for blazing hellfire.

Of course, nowhere in the Bible does it say that *we* have to judge. Thank goodness that's God's job, not ours. But even so, isn't it tacky for the psalmist to lug in all that stuff about wishing sinners wiped out?

I don't know. But here's how I think about it. We notice sin, like wind, only in its effects in the lives of sinners. Maybe what the psalmist wishes here is that sin itself be flushed out of creation's systems.

He's just taken a mental tour of the glorious order and beauty of creation, and he's still pumped up about how beautiful a world God has made. He's so up, in fact, that he can't help but add this one little wish: that there would be no sin; that, in other words, God's kingdom would finally come.

Maybe he's just wishing for heaven. Sometimes, so do I.

Help us to fight the sin that lives in us, and help us fight the sin that grows in the world around us. Sharpen our vision to see the way it darkens the beauty of your world; then send us out to fight. In Jesus' name, Amen.

PSALM 104

HONESTY IV

Some things you just can't tell your parents. Whitney—and the tapes—was one of those things.

Matt knew very well what both of of his parents thought about the Mama's Boys and Brass Thistles. Whenever he'd put them on, he could feel his mom and dad sizzle.

So he knew that if he played his new tapes at home, his parents were sure to ask who they belonged to. Sure as anything, they'd hate for him to buy them. Of course, he could easily tell them the tapes belonged to Whitney. But they weren't too hot on her either because they didn't know her well and they knew her parents didn't go to church—at least not the one they went to.

Matt turned into Lambeth Park, deciding at the last minute to take the shortcut home. As he crossed the wood bridge over the creek, everything rattled, and somehow one of the tapes in his bag slipped out. He reached for it quickly, but with all the bumps it got away from him, slipped between the wires of the basket, bounced once on the bridge, and fell right into the creek below.

Matt dropped his bike in the ditch and ran down the embankment to the thick grass at the edge. He could jump in, he figured, try to feel around with his toes. But he knew right away that the best of the Brass Thistles was gone. No way was he going to fish it out of the stream when he couldn't even see the bottom. He found a stick beside the edge and poked around in the flow, but all he could feel was gritty, heavy sand.

He got down on his haunches at the edge of stream and started to laugh. Here he was all worked up about the stupid tapes, and now some bullhead downstream was going to pick up Brass Thistles and stick it in his Walkman.

Matt fell back against the bank and sat there in the long grass beneath the bridge. Maybe a two-foot carp would snort that tape off the bottom and start into snapping his fins. "Hey, guys," the carp would say, "it's Brass Thistles."

Besides, the stupid tape meant nothing to him. He didn't want it— he'd taken it only to make Whitney feel better. She didn't want it back. He hadn't paid a dime for it. If it was gone, big deal. At least the fish could cut loose.

Matt sat there and laughed so hard that his sides hurt. It was nice to be alone down here—almost like being out in the wilderness. Nothing moved. Nothing challenged him. A guy could almost live down here, Matt thought, start his own place.

Years ago, some teacher had read Matt's class the story of boxcar children—kids who lived on their own, did just what they wanted to. He could do the same thing down here, he thought—live beneath the bridge in Lambeth Park, where no one would ever see him. That'd solve his problem with Whitney.

Like a thin sliver of darkness, a barn swallow swooped past him and swept up to a rafter beneath the bridge. It had to be a barn swallow— Matt could tell by the light gold chest. She sat there dabbing the wet mud at the top of a nest she was building—under the bridge. This was no *barn* swallow, he thought. This was a *bridge* swallow.

There were no barns around Lambeth Park anymore, now that developments were popping up. The swallow probably thought that the bridge was as good a place as any nowadays, so she started a place beneath the bridge, just as he thought about doing himself.

She balanced on the edge of the nest, shaping the ridge with her beak, smoothing it back and forth, rounding it off nicely as if some teacher were about to give her a grade. She seemed to know he was there, but she didn't really care. Whenever he'd move his hand even slightly, her head would jerk quickly, her thin little beak turned toward him. But she didn't fly away.

There was something dark and sleek about the swallow, something thin and rich. Barn swallows are birds people love to watch, he thought. Not like a starling or a crow or a sparrow. Who cares about sparrows? he thought. Nobody really watches the sparrows.

Except God, he remembered.

God's eyes are on the barn swallows, too, he thought. God could find this mom a place to nest, even if the barns were long gone. And he could do the same thing for crummy old sparrows. Even if no one else cared about them, God would.

And if he cared about barn swallows and sparrows, he certainly had time for people—even people who were mixed up or acting crazy.

Matt pulled himself up from the grass, glanced at his watch, and slipped up the side of the embankment. It was time he got home, he thought. The Brass Thistles tape was long gone.

Help us to see your hand in the nests of the barn swallows, in the color of the stormy sky, in the cattle on a thousand hills. Grant us the vision to see your hand in everything around us. That way we'll see you more clearly. Amen.

GIVING

....

Psalm 107:1-3

I'm in trouble. In the next month, I've got to give my wife two gifts—one for our anniversary and another, three weeks later, for her birthday. I won't forget. I've forgotten in the past, and believe me, it won't happen again.

I'm in trouble because buying her a gift is tough. Not so with our kids. I can always pick up another Nintendo game for our son, something with Milly Buzzits and Oopher Goophers to bump off the screen. Some wild T-shirt will thrill our daughter, especially if it's tie-dyed. But what about my wife?

Clothes? A new sweater or a fancy blouse? I've tried that, and sometimes it's worked. But sometimes it hasn't. What looks great on a hanger may be too loose around the midriff or too tight someplace else. Nobody likes to wear things that don't feel good. Maybe she won't like the color—or maybe it won't go with a skirt. I'm skittish about investing in something that she might never take off the closet hanger.

Jewelry? Barbara just isn't into it. Some kind of diamond, I suppose, would thrill her—maybe "shock" is a better word—but she'd feel guilty about my buying it and her wearing it.

Last year I bought her a wok for Chinese cooking. We used it last night to stir-fry onions, green peppers, and beef strips for a Mexican dish, frajitos. It was only the third time the birthday wok had been out of the box—get this!—in an entire year.

We're not filthy rich, but the fact is that my wife usually buys what she needs or wants herself. She checks out catalogs or spends a day in the mall and comes up with something that pleases her. So I could just give her money, I suppose, but that's about as romantic as candlelight over ring baloney.

Chocolates are wonderful, but she's watching her weight. She'd scowl. And although I know her willpower would melt at the sight of red licorice, I'd feel cheap buying her something that only cost a buck and a half.

Flowers are always nice, but every Tom, Dick, and Harry gives flowers. A guy's got to be a little creative.

A food processor? She's not that hot on cooking.

A nice pen? Did that two years ago.

A painting? We've got no wall space.

An accordian? Get serious.

A dog? Then I'll have to walk it every night in January . . . .

As you can see, it's not easy to pick out a gift for my wife. Love, I'm certain, is what she really wants. What it comes packaged in isn't as important as the expression itself. But I can just imagine the expression on her face if on her birthday I'd slip into the family room, sit down beside her, take her hand in mine, and whisper that this year I'm simply giving her my love. The look in her eyes would be memorable. You can bet on it.

I'm glad I don't have to buy gifts for God. He doesn't need a food processor, and no sweater will fit him. Everything belongs to him anyway. He'd be impossible to buy a gift for.

I suppose the only real gift to God—in fact, the only thing we *can* give him—is thanks in praise.

"O give thanks" are the first three words of Psalm 107, a wonderful song of praise.

Thanks is all we can give him—and all he really asks for.

We're so used to paying for things, Lord, that it's hard for us to remember that what you give to us— your love—is free. Thank you so much for your love, for the gift of your Son in our place. I guess we can't say it enough. Amen.

LOST AND FOUND

....
Psalm 107:4-9

What she had seen of Chicago could have been Tulsa or Kansas City: strange faces on dirty sidewalks down a cluttered sidestreet full of cars that rarely moved. Charlotte Baldwin, two thousand miles from her parents' Arizona home, was terribly alone, even though thousands and thousands of people never stopped passing on the freeway above the filthy street where her husband, Richard, had parked the Dodge.

Richard had been gone for almost two days. He'd said he was going to look for a job and someplace to stay. But Richard always made promises he didn't keep. They had come to Chicago—by way of three starving weeks—because Richard said there would be work here, a new life.

Diana, eleven months old, stood beside the wheel and watched a flock of pigeons strut across the street. At least she was still pudgy. Charlotte had spent every last cent they had on milk and food in those weeks of wandering.

"Birdie," Diana said, poking her finger out the window.

Her diaper was sagging—full, again. Charlotte reached behind her seat for the bag, but it was empty. No food and no diapers.

Richard had said he'd be gone for an hour. That was Thursday night. Now it was Saturday morning.

All day Friday Charlotte had watched for him on the sidewalk. She had turned the rearview mirror to be able to keep an eye on the corner behind her where a beer sign flashed off and on even during the day. She'd waited so long. When she had dared, she had walked Diana down the street, just to get out of the car. But Richard had taken the keys, and she didn't dare leave the car— not with everything they owned packed in the trunk and backseat.

Her mother had told her to go with him, even though both of them were afraid of what might happen to Richard—and to them. "I know you will take care of the baby," her mother had said. "And the Lord will take care of you. Always remember to trust in the Lord."

Charlotte was watching Diana when the cop knocked on the top of the car. "You've been here almost two days," he said. "You in trouble, lady? That kid need something to eat?"

What good would it do to lie, she thought. Why should I protect Richard? He's left me so often before. So she told the man about Richard and the job and the two hungry days in the car in a city where she was a stranger.

The policeman took Charlotte and Diana to a shelter—a place where Charlotte could watch her hungry baby drink cold fresh milk and eat cereal; a place where Charlotte was served eggs and sausage that tasted like a queen's breakfast.

"You know," she told the policeman, "God sent you to me. He takes care of us. I always trust in him."

Charlotte Baldwin's story—and this is only one of them—is the story of Psalm 107, a story of wandering and homelessness, but also a story of God's loving hands always protecting those he loves. He won't break his promises, even when others do.

You're always there to take us back, dear Lord, even
if we've run away from you. Your love for us is a
wonder. Be with us in every chapter of our lives.
Amen.

FOR SWEETHEARTS AND REBELS

....
Psalm 107:4-32

Henry Ford made a Model A and a bundle of money. But what some people remember most about him is something he said—a line that was printed in the *Chicago Tribune* on May 25, 1916: "History is more or less bunk."

Most school kids likely agree with Ford. Perhaps history becomes interesting only after you've accumulated some yourself.

The Jews, God's chosen people, certainly accumulated some history: you can read about it in the Old Testament. Even today, when Jewish people celebrate the Passover, they celebrate their history as a people.

Psalm 107 reads like a hymn, complete with stanzas and choruses. The first four verses remind the people to thank God for his blessings. The next five (vv. 5-9) tell a story of a wandering people who find a home once they cry out to God for help. Verses 10-16 draw a picture of people who've gotten themselves in big trouble and finally ask God to help them. The next section (vv. 17-22) describes people who've become sick because of sin, and the following ten verses (vv. 23-32) tell us of rebellious sailors who return to God. In each section rebels turn to God, and he rescues them.

Verses 33-42 present a whole list of things that God has done for his people, and the psalm ends with a tidy little lesson to all of us: if you're smart, don't forget that God remembers.

The Jewish people had no problem understanding this psalm because it echoed their history. For instance, wandering in the desert wasteland (v. 4) reminded them of the long struggle for a home in Canaan, and the prisoner (v. 10) reminded them of their years of bondage in Egypt and Babylon. So this very structured song—full of stories and choruses—is something of a hymn of history for the Jewish people.

I'm not Jewish. I'm Dutch-American. The psalm might be interesting if you're into Jewish history or if you're Jewish yourself, but if you're not—who cares? History is bunk.

Well, hold on. I may not be an Israeli, but I sure enough am one of God's chosen people. And since I am, the story of his people is my story too. It's my history.

I know people who've wandered, who've gotten themselves in trouble, and who were rescued by God—people who were believers.

The fact is, the stories in this psalm—and the ones I know—aren't pleasant. Several of them are about believers who walked out on God. That happens. You know it, and I know it.

But the whole point of the song is that all of us—the sweethearts and the rebels—better learn that only God hears us when we cry, and only he can deliver us.

He doesn't quit when we do. That's history.

Dear Lord, there's nothing new about your love. We read all about it in the Bible. We know you'll be our God because we know your promise to your people. Thank you for the gift of life eternal. Amen.

THE PRODIGAL

Psalm 107:43

I've been thinking about Jerelyn Comisky. You may remember her. I dreamed her up for a story about feeling forsaken by God. Her parents were separating, and she had seen her dad with some flashy girl about half his age. Jerelyn doesn't exist, of course. I made her up. But you and I both know Jerelyns. In fact, you may be one of them.

Because God's people live with him for eternity, the lives of Christians always have good endings. But that doesn't mean that stories about Christians always end with people hugging each other and singing "Jesus Loves Me." Long chapters of some Christians' stories are bad, some of them X-rated. For a while John Newton, the man who wrote the hymn "Amazing Grace," was a slave-trader—he bought and sold human flesh. Then God rescued him, and we remember him today not for his sins but for that great song.

But I've been thinking about Jerelyn. Obviously, she's no villain. She and her mother and sisters have been mistreated by her dad (in the story I made up). He's the one who left them behind.

Let's assume for a minute—and this is tough—that her dad is a Christian. Now I know you'll say that Christians don't pull the kind of stunts this guy pulled, but sometimes they do. David did. He picked Bathsheba right out of her bathtub, then had her husband killed. So it's not unusual for Christians to sin badly; I wish it weren't that way, but it is. If you don't know that already, you'll learn it someday soon—and when you do, it'll hurt.

I want you to imagine Jerelyn's father the night she saw him in King Crab with some dipsie-doodle girl half his age. Jerelyn went right home and cried, remember? But what did *he* do? Let's just imagine for awhile. Let's let him talk.

"I left Felicia's apartment early, not because of the look on Jerelyn's face but because I wondered what I must have looked like to her—with Felicia. 'Dirt,' she'd probably say. I can't think of anything low enough, really.

"The streets were already empty when I drove home. I kept the radio up high to keep noise in my head, but I was thinking about the first time I'd taken Jerelyn up in the plane and how she'd looked over the city, picked out our house, and told me how different everything looked from up there. 'This is what God sees,' she said. She was four, I think—not even in school.

"When I got back to my apartment, I snapped on the lights, looked around, and started to clean. From the first day I had moved in here, I'd told myself I wasn't going to let things go to pot. I didn't want to come home to a place that was as messed up as I was. But that night as I looked around at the spotless cupboards, at the mail lined up perfectly on the desk, at the pillows stacked in the corners of the couch, it seemed as if no one really lived here.

"I want you to understand that I felt as if there were no me that night, as if I'd disappeared into some strange warp. I felt invisible, as if this wasn't home. And I guess it isn't.

"I hadn't prayed for three months. That night I did. But I was scared."

Psalm 107, a history of God's people, contains a log of stories about people who turn their backs on God for a while.

Jerelyn's dad is not my favorite character, but God's people aren't always squeaky clean. God takes us back just the same.

Forgive us for walking away from you, for forgetting
you, or for deliberately turning our backs on you for
some silly reason. We're all guilty before your face.
Thank you for freeing us from our sins through Jesus
Christ. Amen.

PSALM 107

HONESTY V

"I clean 'em," Whitney said, pointing at a small apartment complex. "People move out, and my dad pays me to clean up their mess." She flashed a key. "You wouldn't believe what they leave behind. Once I got a perfectly good TV. Some other junk too— a tennis racket and stuff."

Maybe he was wrong about her, Matt thought. Maybe she'd just picked up tapes some renters left behind. Maybe she didn't steal them after all. He wondered if she'd ever given anything to the others who were with them. To Brad or to Mike or to her friend Shelley.

"Let's go in," Mike said, pointing at the building.

Whitney flashed the key again. "I can get in any apartment I want," she said. "I've been in all of them."

The sun was just going down, so it was that time of night when things are dim, too dim to read much more than the "Now Renting" banner over the name of the complex.

"One of 'ems empty," she said. "I know because I got to clean it tomorrow."

Matt looked at his watch. It was Friday—his parents would be expecting him home. Besides, he wasn't too sure about sneaking into an apartment. "You sure it's empty?" he said. "You can't just walk in someplace, even if your dad owns it."

Whitney shrugged her shoulders. "I know which one."

No one was around, so the five teenagers walked up the side stairs to the second floor. Matt figured it wouldn't look good at all if someone saw this whole pack of kids going into one of the apartments, even if the place was empty.

"I'm sure it's 211," she said. When she stuck the master key into the door, it opened to darkness. She snapped on the light without going in. "This is it," she said, "look."

The furniture was still there, but all the cupboard doors were thrown open. A stack of newspapers stood against the wall by the refrigerator beside five grocery bags of empty 7-Up cans.

"There's nothing here," Matt said. "Junk—that's all."

But Mike was already inside, looking in the corners. "Check this out," he said, and he held up a blue cap that said "Sweet Port Beer" in silver lettering. "There's dozens of 'em."

All sorts of beer junk lay in a pile just beyond the couch: caps, frisbees, socks, sunglasses—all with Port Beer logos.

"You sure nobody lives here?" Matt asked.

Whitney said she was positive this was the place she had to clean. She leaned out the door and checked the number again.

She was probably right, Matt thought. All someone had left behind was the advertising junk. And since Whitney would be dumping all of this stuff when she cleaned, they might as well help themselves.

"We look like we're in a beer commercial," Shelley giggled, as they left the apartment ten minutes later. Matt had pulled on a pair of Sweet Port socks. Mike wore shades with "Sweet Port" inscribed lightly on the lenses. And they all wore Sweet Port hats.

"This key gets me into every apartment," Whitney said.

Matt didn't like her talking that loud, but it was obvious that she thought she was really big-time now.

"Think we can find something else?" Mike asked.

Whitney stopped and put her finger to her lips to tell them to keep down the noise. Here and there lights burned, but other than the hum from a stereo playing somewhere on the other side of the building, everything seemed quiet.

"Come on," Mike said. "Let's look around."

When you're with a bunch of kids like that, you don't dare say much. Matt looked at Shelley—and then at the others, but nobody said anything. So when Whitney signaled with her hand, they all followed her slowly around the corner to 216. She looked around once again, then slipped in the key.

"I know the guy," Whitney said. "He works nights."

So many hamburger wrappers and empty cups lay around the apartment that it looked like a Burger Barn dump. Half-read magazines lay beside the TV, along with dozens of cassettes.

Matt felt like he shouldn't be there. It was as if he were prying into someone's secrets. His heart was banging like hiccups. "What's there to see anyway?" he asked. "It's a pigpen."

"What a world," Mike said. "Nothing but burgers." He walked to the kitchen along a path cut through the junk.

"Gives me the shakes," Matt said. "Let's go."

"Six-pack of Coke—that's it," Mike said, looking in the fridge. "A whole big refrigerator for a six lousy Cokes." He pulled them out. "Let's drink 'em," he said.

Whitney snapped out the light. "Put on some music," she said. "I'm thirsty."

"You sure he works?" Matt asked.

"I know the guy," Whitney said. In the dark her voice came out of nothing more than a silhouette. "Let's party."

When our reputation is at stake, it's easy to turn our backs on what we know is right. We want so badly to be accepted, but you accept us the way we are. Even though we're sinners, you take us to be your children. Amen.

DAVID'S EXAMPLE

....

Psalm 51

Chad went away to college and fell in love—hard, as if he'd fallen from the top of Grand Coulee Dam. He spent hours with Carrie, and when he was alone, she was all he thought about. Don't laugh. It happens.

When semester exams came around, a kid in Chad's dorm got the answers for the math test. Chad couldn't study anything but Carrie 101. He figured the only chance he had of making it through the test was using stolen answers. He did. He got caught.

Then he got thrown out of school.

Carrie was heartbroken. Chad's parents nearly had a fit. And Chad felt like a mud ball. So he prayed as he'd never prayed before. "It was really stupid," he told God. "I'm really sorry. I should never have done it. I know it."

Maybe you remember doing something really wrong. If you did, you probably prayed harder than you ever had before.

David took Bathsheba as his wife, then knocked off Uriah, her husband, as if he were a bug. Once Nathan explained what David had done, he felt rotten—probably worse than Chad did.

But David's prayer is different from Chad's. Psalm 51 is actually a little strange. After all, here's David on his knees praying for forgiveness, and he doesn't even mention Bathsheba or Uriah—except in one word, *bloodguilt*, in verse 14.

David may have been an ordinary guy when it came to sex, but he was no ordinary believer—and no ordinary pray-er. He starts this psalm by asking for mercy, but then he gives a kind of shorthand testimony: "Have mercy on me, O God, according to your unfailing love," he says. Instead of just begging forgiveness for what he did, David tells God that he believes, completely, that God's love never fails. He knows he can be forgiven.

Then he says something really strange: "Against you, you only, have I sinned." Uriah would have had a right to feel a little testy if he'd heard that.

But David knew that sinning against another person pales in comparison with doing something to hurt God Almighty. Hurting God is even worse than murder.

It's possible, I think, that some death-row convicts are more alarmed about being strapped to an electric chair than they are about the murders they have committed. But not David. "Wash away all my iniquity," he says, because he knows that sin is a condition, like a disease.

That's why he says later, "Create in me a pure heart." Only God *creates* things. By asking him to *create* a new heart, David admits his heart is as rotten as an old, wet ceiling joist. He begs God to start over, to wash him inside and out, to rid him of the whole condition of sin.

David admits that his sin showed he was rotten to the core. That's why he needs God's forgiveness.

Actually, the psalm serves as an example to people like Chad—and all of us. We all have sinned. It's not just the really, really dirty things we do that need forgiveness.

We need to be created anew. Only God can do that job.

When we're really down, Lord, when we're in real
trouble, you will still forgive—even when nobody
else will. Thank you for rebuilding our lives and our
hearts. Amen.

YES, YOU, DAVID

....

2 Samuel 12:1-14

The story of David and Bathsheba has already been made into a movie, of course, but if I were a millionaire, I'd do it again.

Which Hollywood actor wouldn't want David's part: God's own chosen king, a powerful man who ran Israel with equal doses of strength and mercy? I could get anybody.

For that matter, what actress could stay away from the role of Bathsheba? The name itself is a scandal.

But it's the part of Nathan I like best in this story. I like to picture him as a real John-the-Baptist type—a scraggly character, a windblown, dust-driven weirdo munching on grasshoppers he picks and eats, two or three at a time, from a leather pouch. To me, he has occult eyes, crystals that shine like live planets. And although he never says much, when you're in a room with him, you catch yourself thinking that he's reading whatever is printed inside your head.

I picture Nathan's scene something like this: The prophet comes in and refuses to be seated. What he's got to say won't come off the way it should from a love seat or a fainting couch. When he talks, he uses his hands to tell the story about a rich man who for no good reason at all slaughtered the lamb of a poor man—in fact, the only lamb the poor man had.

Nathan's nostrils flare, his eyes shine, his voice lowers, even quivers. And when he's finished telling the story, silence sits in the room like an uninvited guest.

David is overwhelmed by the injustice. He swallows hard, as if allowing his vengeance any space would be to risk sin itself.

"Who is it? Do I know the jackal? Tell me who he is, and I'll have him dressed out like a side of beef," David says, standing himself now, roaring mad.

Nathan waits, still staring. Slowly, he drops his hands to his sides, and out of nowhere he flashes a jeweled hand mirror, round and shiny. This time, when Nathan speaks, his voice is solemn, but perfectly clear, his words emerging as if they were being played on the world's oldest pipe organ.

"You are the man, David," Nathan says.

David's face petrifies.

The wind rises, lifting the curtains from the windows.

"Here's what the Lord says," Nathan tells him. "I would have given you anything, but you took what wasn't yours. Now you will suffer. For what you have done, the son born to Bathsheba will die. You have sinned."

David doesn't try to deny anything. He doesn't accuse Nathan of showing up at the wrong address. Somewhere in the palace Bathsheba is right now looking over her summer dresses, and he knows there's no room anywhere for him to hide from the voice that he understands doesn't come from this fleabag prophet.

The voice, he knows, belongs to his God—the one who chose him to be king, the one who allowed him to deliver his people from the terror of Goliath, the one who empowered him to be a man of God.

"I have sinned against the Lord," David says. That's all.

Some movies can be replayed over and over and over again.

Dear God, sometimes it's hard for us to recognize our own sins. We're experts at the art of cover-up. Help us to see clearly what we've done wrong—and just as clearly show us forgiveness and hope. We know that you love us. Amen.

A MOTHER'S GUILT

....

Psalm 51:1-6

A twenty-year-old named Jennifer Gardner was murdered not long ago in a city near my home in Iowa. Two brothers strangled her while she was watching TV. The papers say that there must have been some kind of fight first, some argument that angered the boys.

Jennifer was living with an older brother of the murderers. She had what some people call "a checkered past," in and out of lockups all over the country, constantly in trouble with the law. She'd met her boyfriend in jail somewhere. And when she died, she was working as an exotic dancer.

Jennifer had no home, really. The papers say her mother never cared about her at all, and her father disappeared long ago. She was born into the world, but never had parents.

The boys who killed her will be punished—the oldest one, just seventeen, will be tried as an adult, the papers say this morning. Iowa has no death penalty, but you can bet that the courts will throw the book at him—and his little brother.

What's most sad about the whole business is my suspicion that this young girl seemed almost destined to die a violent and horrible death. She's not to blame for her own murder, of course, but her short life seemed pointed toward something just this awful. She probably never had much love.

In a way, I guess, I blame her parents. They deserve some stiff sentence themselves.

In California, courts ruled recently that parents should be responsible for the crimes of their children. Authorities arrested a woman who allegedly allowed her son to hang around with a violent street gang. She's being charged for negligence because of *his* crimes.

Can a son's crime really be his mother's—or father's—fault? That's a tough question.

When David says, in verse 5, "Surely I was . . . sinful from the time my mother conceived me," he isn't accusing his mother of anything. We really know very little of David's mother, except that she was married to a good man, Jesse, and together with him had eight sons, of which David was the baby. We have no reason to think she was a dishonorable woman.

And David does not mean to blame her for the whole stinky Bathsheba affair. What he means to tell the Lord is that he recognizes very clearly that the sins he's just committed, the ones that he's been found guilty of, are not just quirky exceptions. He wants God to clean house on him because he's been—like all of us—prone to look away from God since the day he was conceived. Sin is an old part of his life.

Ugly as that makes him, dirty as he seems, David knows God's faithfulness will make him new—as it can do for all of us, for Jennifer Gardner, and even for the boys who killed her.

The incredible thing about God's love is that it makes the rottenest characters squeaky clean. God's love is unfailing.

Help us not to blame others for our problems, but to acknowledge our weaknesses and our failures. Strengthen us through the love that only you can give. In your Son's name, Amen.

BLOODGUILT

....
Psalm 51:7-19

My wife hasn't gone biking by herself since the day—more than a month ago—when she fell and put a gash in her head the size and shape of fork's tines. I don't blame her. I'm not sure *I've* recovered.

When I picked up the phone that day, a sweet little voice announced I should come to the hospital's emergency room. "Your wife asked if you'd come down," the voice said. "She's had a little fall."

Some little fall.

When I got there, a woman from the rescue squad was pressing a bloody cloth to Barbara's face. The plastic brace they'd set around her neck jerked her chin up awkwardly. Deep purple made her eyes look like an inkwell. But the worst was the blood.

Blood flows from facial cuts the way sugar pours from a torn bag. Barbara's jacket was soaked, her hair was clotted, and her neck seemed caked. An ambulance attendant told me she had also left a bright scarlet wading pool on the blacktop where she'd fallen. I couldn't help wondering how much of her allotted five quarts was still meandering through her system.

She's over it now. A concussion kept her dizzy longer than she cared to be, but now the twelve-stitch scar is getting pink, and her major-league black eye has played out its overture of colors.

About a week ago we took our bikes past the spot where she went down. I'd told her that her blood had stained the road where she'd fallen—two, foot-wide pools like binoculars set on end.

She didn't believe it. But she was wrong. Rain has come and gone since that day, but the stain is still there.

Blood. Nothing is quite so red, not even a rose. Nothing is so crucial, not even the air we breathe. Nothing shocks us so powerfully when it's spilled, and nothing stays with us like the sight of it left behind. I say *blood*, and you see it, smell it, even feel it. Ask Stephen King how important it is in a story.

In Psalm 51, David refers specifically to what he's done with only one word, *bloodguilt*. He's suffering from guilt, but not just any kind— bloodguilt.

The guilt David feels is bloodguilt's India-ink stain. It just won't wash away.

In Shakespeare's *Macbeth,* Lady Macbeth urges her husband to kill Duncan in order to gain the crown. He does it, but when it's over, he turns to jello, fidgeting at every little noise, scared of his own shadow.

Lady Macbeth tells him to grab hold of himself and wash the blood off his hands. "A little water clears us of this deed," she says, smoothly. "How easy is it, then?"

She's absolutely wrong, of course. By the end of the play, she's wandering around the palace rubbing her hands tortuously, as if the stain were still there. Bloodguilt drove her insane.

David knew his bloodguilt would never disappear without God's great forgiveness. "Save me from bloodguilt, O God, the God who saves me," he says, "and my tongue will sing of your righteousness" (v. 14).

He knows. It hurts him to know himself, but it thrills him to know God, because only God can cleanse him fully from his sin.

"O God," he says, "you will not despise."

If we were to live forever, dear Father in heaven, we could never repay you for your forgiveness and love. May our lives sing your praise. Amen.

PSALM 51

HONESTY VI

The blue light of the television cast shadows in the darkness. Outside the window, anybody walking by could see that dim glow against the curtains, Matt thought.

But they sat there anyway, watching TV and drinking Coke. Whitney sat on a stack of newspapers, Shelley right there beside her, almost as if she were afraid. Brad kept switching the channels with every commercial, and Matt lay across the love seat with his arm up over the pillows as if he weren't afraid. Mike kept snooping around, trying to find something interesting.

"The guy that lives here must be incredibly gross," Shelley said. "These french fries are a year old. What does he do?"

"He doesn't drink," Mike said, poking his head out of the bedroom. "I thought maybe I could find a bottle."

That's all they needed was some beer or something, Matt thought—there'd be trouble for sure.

"He's not a bad guy really," Whitney said.

"But what does he do?" Shelley said. "I mean, it's so dirty—yuck."

Whitney shrugged her shoulders.

"You really *know* this guy?" Matt asked.

"I'm telling you, I do. You think I'd just break into some apartment around here? My dad owns the place, ya know."

"What'd you find, Mike?" Brad yelled.

"Magazines." The answer came from the bedroom.

"What kind?"

"What kind you think?" he said, and Brad took off.

"How long we going to stay?" Matt asked.

"He's here during the day," Whitney said. "I see him all the time—whenever I'm here. I'm telling you, he works nights. It's no big deal. He's a good guy."

"BINGO," Mike yelled, and when he came out of the bedroom he was carrying a bottle of whiskey and an arm full of magazines.

And right at that moment, the cops came . . . .

Sitting in the police station, Matt felt as if his stomach had emptied into his feet, as if there were nothing there under his heart. There they sat in their new beer caps, Mike's booze and magazines on the cop's desk.

Matt's dad's face looked hot enough to steam, and his mother kept a handkerchief up at her eyes the whole time, even though she never cried out loud. It was awful.

"We've had break-ins in that area on and off since last fall," the cop said. "You guys want to tell us about any others you might have been responsible for—or you really want me to believe that this was just a one-time shot?"

Matt and the others looked to Whitney and waited. She had told the man right away that her dad owned the apartments, but that didn't seem to change anything. "I swear we never did this before," she told him. "I swear. I was going to get them to help me clean that apartment, Dad." She turned to him across the room. "I could have done the whole thing with them." Her eyes were streaked with blue from the lines tears cut through her mascara. "Besides, I know him. His name is Roy—Elroy, I think."

"She's right," her father said. "You know that."

Matt's father couldn't look him straight in the eye. Even though the police never talked to him, his father kept his eyes down along the floor while he held Matt's mother's hand.

Everything about what happened looked so bad. They'd broken in, they'd taken the booze and the magazines—and all of them in their stupid beer caps. He couldn't have thought up anything worse. But he knew that if he let himself think about it too long, he would cry. Mike wasn't crying. Brad was—so were his folks. Shelley too. But not Whitney and not him.

"They hadn't stolen anything yet, of course," the cop said to the parents. "It's lucky maybe that we got there when we did. Now it's only breaking and entering."

What was so amazing is that all of it happened so quickly. Matt started thinking about court and probation and all of that, what it might be like to sit in jail. He swallowed hard as the cop got up from the desk and walked around the room.

In his head, he talked to God. *Make it go away,* he said. *It's a bad dream, and it's got to go away.* He'd have a criminal record, he thought. *I'm sorry I did it,* he said, his eyes open. *You can't believe how sorry I am.*

"Talk to God," Adkins had told him. "Tell him everything."

So he did. While his mother rubbed her eyes and his father stared at the floor, Matt just talked and talked and talked, even though he never said a word out loud.

....

Even in the worst times, Lord, keep us talking. Help us to be honest with you, to talk, to tell you every-thing because you are our God and Maker. Amen.

SURVIVOR'S SYNDROME

....

Psalm 42

Psalm 42 is one of seven psalms which, according to the note above its words, was the property of the "sons of Korah," a family of Israelites appointed by David to serve in the temple as priests, those who conducted worship for the people.

The title "sons of Korah" is interesting because Korah's story (in Numbers 16) is one of those totally grizzly Old Testament stories that we'd sometimes rather not read. But let's go over it again, just to see who's singing this psalm.

Think back on Moses and on the Israelites' long trek through the wilderness. After an earlier rebellion, you might remember, God had told Moses that an entire generation of his people would have to die before anyone would get to the promised land. The idea of wandering around in hot sand for another umpteen years—only to die there—couldn't have been very appealing to the men and women of Israel.

Korah definitely wasn't pleased by the idea of wasting his life in the desert. He was a Levite, someone chosen for temple duties—a honcho really, someone with power, no ordinary guy. But Korah decided that the power he'd been given in the temple didn't measure up to his own dreams. So he buttered up two hundred and fifty other malcontents and dragged them along with him to visit Moses.

Korah told the man chosen by God as ruler that the Israelite nation was full of fine people and that Moses had no right to lord it over folks who were just as good as he was. Korah's whole argument was a lie, of course. He wasn't concerned about the people of Israel—only about himself. *He* wanted to be the kingpin, and he was tired of having to follow orders from Moses. Moses put him to the test. "Come around tomorrow with your censors lit," he said, "and we'll see who the Lord wants to rule his people."

Here comes the ugliness. The next morning God himself told Moses and the others to separate themselves from Korah's tents. Moses, fearing the worst, fell down on his face and asked God not to kill off the whole bunch. "Only one of them is really bad," he told God. "Please be careful with the others."

But God made the earth yawn and inhale Korah and all two hundred and fifty others who'd rebelled against Moses. God did exactly what Moses said he would: he made his choice.

We often wince at the horror of such Old Testament stories—an earthquake literally swallowing people alive. But somehow God's ways have their own logic.

This wonderful psalm is sung by Korah's descendants, survivors of that massacre. "I will yet praise him—my Savior and my God." You might think that Korah's kin would be bitter, angry toward God, but apparently they weren't. They sang the praises of God almighty.

We're survivors too, in a way. We've been chosen to live. We can sing the songs of the sons of Korah right along with them.

....

Sometime the old stories of the Bible seem far from real, Lord, but we know that they tell us how you deal with your people. We know that your Word is the story of your promises to us, and we thank you for it from the bottom of our souls. Amen.

THE GOLDEN OLDIES

....

Psalm 42

Our family is the proud owner of two old psalters, two fat little Dutch books that hold the New Testament and musical arrangements of the psalms that Dutch people used to sing.

One of these books belonged to my great-grandmother Dirkse, a woman who spent her whole life in Oostburg, Wisconsin, my hometown. The other belonged to my wife's great-grandmother Haarsma, who died after nearly one hundred years out here on the prairie in Iowa.

The two psalters are almost identical. Both have dark brown leather covers and pages with gold edging that has been worn down to a dusty buff. Both have cracked bindings and lots of loose pages.

It's interesting how both fall open to Psalm 68, a psalm that must have been a favorite with both great-grandmothers, even though they never worshiped together or even knew each other. And in both, the pages of Psalm 42 are thin, stained, and worn.

I'm told that Psalm 42, like Psalm 68, was a great favorite with the Dutch Calvinist immigrants who came to America before 1900. It's not hard to figure out why.

Immigration was no breeze. Most people who came to America at the turn of the century—Dutch, Irish, German, French—had no money. What brought them was the opportunity to work and be free to worship as they pleased. But life wasn't easy.

Maybe when they sang Psalm 42, verse 4, they remembered the old country: "These things I remember as I pour out my soul: how I used to go with the multitude, leading the procession to the house of God, with shouts of joy and thanksgiving."

The psalmist wasn't talking about worship in the Netherlands, of course, but his words may have changed color a little in the loneliness of men and women plowing through a hard life and sometimes remembering what seemed like the good old days.

Likewise, verse 6: "My soul is downcast within me; therefore I will remember you from the land of Jordan, the heights of Hermon—from Mount Mizar." Great-grandma Haarsma never got near the Jordan, but when she sang that phrase, she might well have been thinking of the naked plains of Iowa.

Going to church back then was, for most immigrants, the only break from work. For these people who had no high school basketball, no videos, and no Baskin-Robbins, church services provided an opportunity to rest, to see friends, and to sing together. Church was *the* place to go. So Grandmas Dirkse and Haarsma probably enjoyed reading the psalmist's memories about going to the house of the Lord. They may well have smiled just thinking of church.

But I like to think that the most important reason for both of these old psalters looking old and used at Psalm 42 is the chorus—repeated again, by the way, at the end of Psalm 43: Why are you so sad, my soul? Put your hope in God.

Yep. That's the verse they wanted and needed to hear.

Faith is not something that runs in the genes like baldness or the ability to lick your nose with your tongue. But I like to think that the faith and hope our grandmothers celebrated in that verse still lives in the hearts of grandchildren they never knew.

Maybe I'm silly, but sometimes so is faith itself.

....

We're thankful, Lord, for what your word means to us and what it meant to our grandparents. May its message always stay with us—every hour of every day of our lives. Amen.

DAVID'S CAVE

....
Psalm 42:8-11

Way back when, somebody named a small mountain range east of Phoenix, Arizona, the Superstitions. One has only to see these mountains to understand why.

Standing above a forest of saguaro cacti, the Superstitions are a tangle of odd shapes, buttressed by red cliffs. Somewhere in the middle of the range, a lone weather-worn rock, split in the center, stands like a monument. People call it the Weaver's Needle. You may have seen pictures of it.

But it isn't only the odd appearance of the Superstitions that has given these mountains their name. It's also the legends that people have created about this unusual range. Some say people have been known to wander into these mountains and simply disappear, as if the Superstitions were the hideaway of silent terrorists or the headquarters for a spaceship of aliens. Others believe that hidden in the rugged range is a million-dollar gold mine, The Lost Dutchman, the secret of some whacky prospector who never whispered its whereabouts but got fabulously wealthy on the goods he carved out of the rock.

The Superstitions hold their mysteries well, even today. A century ago they were the stronghold of renegade Apache Indians, led by their famous chief, Cochise. If you hike through the Superstitions today, you probably won't find the old Dutchman's map or his million-dollar gold mine, but you *will* stumble upon a high, stony fortress known, and marked, as Cochise's Cave.

Here, the story goes, Cochise and his men found sanctuary from their enemies, the white soldiers who were ordered into the Superstitions to hunt down the last of Arizona's warring natives.

I've been in Cochise's Cave, and I'll never forget the place. In fact, being in that Indian chief's cave helped me to understand what the psalmist means when he claims that the Lord is his stronghold—or his rock, as David says in verse 9. I'd probably read that line (and sung it) a thousand times without any clear idea of what it meant. The strength and safety of "rock" isn't clear, really, to people who live in the suburbs. But Cochise would have known what the psalmist meant—and so would the United States Cavalry.

If you can, try to imagine the largest hamburger in the world, a monster that stands up above the land. The meat in the middle we'll call the cave. Now imagine that Cochise's men are in that cave, a room big enough to hold a roaring fire. Think of that as the Apaches' sanctuary.

Cochise stands at the entry to his lair and looks for miles over stony crags and valleys. If there is a plume of dust anywhere within sight, he sees it. So no one can take the place from the front. But no one can take the place from behind, either: the top of the hamburger bun is sheer cliff.

I remember standing at the mouth of Cochise's Cave and thinking that the place must have been invincible. The signs call it Cochise's Cave, but it's a rock and a half.

Psalm 42 says the Lord is a rock, a fortress that can't be taken, a sanctuary that can't be stormed. When you're in the Lord, you're safe.

In trouble and problems, in life and in death, you,
Lord, are the place we can go for help and assurance.
You are our comfort, our rock. Thank you for being
the Lord of our lives. Thank you for your Son. In his
name, Amen.

BEING AWAY

....
Psalm 43

Psalms 42 and 43 are songs about being away and not liking it. You might say they're songs that prove that absence makes the heart grow fonder. You *might* say that.

I tested out that theory once in my life, and I lost—well, maybe I won. My high school sweetheart and I decided to go to different colleges, hundreds of miles apart. If we were somehow "supposed" to stay together, we thought, we would. Absence, I figured, would make my heart grow fonder.

We wrote each other a lot and made it through most of both semesters. Then writing became a chore, and the letters got dry as bone. They failed to start my heart a-flutterin'. I'm sure she'd say the same thing. In this case, the old line about absence proved itself as accurate as the *National Enquirer*.

Maybe the exception proves the rule. I know a guy who came back from China and claimed that when he was there, he would have surrendered his Nike Airs for a Big Mac and a large order of fries.

But the Bible isn't written to prove the truth of folk wisdom or psychological principle. The moral of these psalms is not that absence makes the heart grow fonder. The God the psalmist misses, after all, is not a high school sweetheart or plastic-wrapped fast food—it's Jehovah, the great I AM.

Just a word here about the Old Testament. To Israel, God *lived* in Jerusalem. I know people who think he lives in Grand Rapids, Michigan, but most of us know that the only place he calls home today is the souls of his people. We have no main temple in Nova Scotia or New Mexico. Our God doesn't have a street address or keep office hours.

But the psalmist's horrible distress isn't due just to being away from home—or the temple, for that matter. It's more than that.

What's behind the psalmist's longing is his feeling that God just simply can't be found. Somehow, believes the psalmist, God must have misplaced his people—or worse, rejected them (43:2). So it's not just being away from God's temple that makes the psalmist weep; it's being away from God, left behind, forgotten. It's not absence, but rejection.

I must admit something to you. I've never felt that way. Life's been pretty easy for me, I guess. Maybe if I'd been one of the skinny survivors of Auschwitz, I'd wonder about where God was. Maybe if my family had been killed in some freakish crash, I'd wonder if I had been forgotten. Maybe if the bomb someday blows, I'll look up and see a sky with nothing beyond it.

But if anything like that ever happens to me, at least I'll know Psalm 42, which teaches me this: that when the Israelites felt God had checked out of their world, abandoned them like a scared kid on a downtown city street full of strangers, they still held to their faith. Psalm 42 will help me.

"I will *yet* praise him," these psalms repeat, time and time again. "I will *yet* praise him." That's like a pledge. Despite my feeling forgotten, "I will *yet* praise him."

I swear, he's never gone. Thanks, Psalm 42.

In the times in our lives when we feel left behind by friends and family and even by you, Lord, stay with us and comfort us. Give us strength to trust in you.
Amen.

PSALMS 42 & 43

HONESTY VII

When the apartment owner named Elroy walked in, Matt thought he looked cleaner than he should have. He wore an over-sized white cotton shirt, jeans, and loafers with no socks. He had a belly on him big enough to curl over his belt and make him a little older than he tried to look. And he seemed cocky, as if this weren't the cop shop at all. Of course, he wasn't the one in trouble.

"Whitney," he said, "they tell me you guys were having a party at my place." His whole belly lurched when he laughed.

"You're Elroy?" the cop asked.

He nodded his head.

A policewoman came in behind him with a clipboard under her arm. "He finally showed up," she said.

Matt had been sure Whitney was lying about her friendship with Elroy. But here the guy was, and he had picked Whitney right out of the group, even said her name.

Elroy reached into his pocket and pulled out a stick of gum, unwrapped it, and stuck it in his mouth. "You owe me a couple of Cokes I hear," he said. "I hope you cleaned the place up a little." He sat back on the desk, as if it were his.

Whitney didn't say a word, and that wasn't like her at all.

"I don't know what you're holding these kids for," Elroy said to the cops. "Whitney told me already Tuesday that she'd be up. I was a kid once. You all were. They got no place to go—you know what I'm saying?" He turned the aluminum foil into a ball between his fingers and dropped it in an ashtray on the desk. "I'm not going to press no charges," he said. "You can't hardly mess up that place worse than it is. I ought to get married or som̲et̲h̲i̲n̲g—get somebody to keep the place clean."

He tried to make it a joke, but nobody laughed.

But that was all the excuse the five teenagers needed. The cops had no choice but to send them home . . . .

It was almost like a miracle, Matt thought, sitting in the backseat by himself. Things had looked awful for awhile, but then this guy Elroy showed up and lied them right out of it. Out of nowhere.

"There's something strange about the whole business," his dad said. "It sticks in my craw somehow. I don't like it."

Matt and his parents were on their way home, and nobody had really said much because there wasn't anything to say. Matt hadn't been drinking—the cops even said that—and what they'd done turned out to be okay. What was there to say?

"You heard the guy," Matt said.

"You know him?" his mom asked.

"I never saw him before."

The interior flashed bright and dim as they passed beneath the string of streetlights on the long avenue up to their house. Matt knew very well what his dad meant. It *was* strange. It made no sense that this Elroy would lie the way he had. Whitney had never told him they'd be in there. She couldn't have.

"I'll say this much," his dad said. "He saved your hides."

That was true, of course. Matt had stuck his stupid beer cap in a wastebasket on his way out because he knew that his parents wouldn't take to it, especially after what had happened.

"I think we ought to ground you just the same," his dad said. "I mean, something's bad here, even if I can't put my finger on it."

"They didn't really harm anyone," his mother said.

"I know, but something stinks."

Matt wished he could tell them everything, but he just couldn't. "I'm sorry," he said.

"What for?" his dad asked. "I want to know why."

He didn't know exactly. They stopped at a four-way and waited for a street cleaner. It wasn't even eleven. "Just for making you go to the station. I mean, I feel bad that you had to come down there and get me—"

"Something's rotten," his dad said. "Stay away from it, Matt," he said. "Just stay clear."

"Do you like Whitney?" his mother asked.

He didn't know how to answer that one. Maybe his whole fear that she had been stealing was stupid. But after tonight he was somehow even more afraid, and he didn't know why. "She's like a friend," he said, "you know. I mean, I don't *like* her, like you mean *like*."

When his mother didn't say anything back to him, he knew that she had meant the question as a warning.

"Am I getting punished?" Matt asked.

"Your father and I will talk it over."

Matt had to keep it all inside. He hated to, but he had to. There was no choice. He couldn't tell anyone about Whitney and the stealing and all the questions he had. He might just as well have been the only human being on earth, because he couldn't tell a soul.

Sometimes it feels as if we're just going to explode,
Lord. It seems that there's so much inside that we
can't contain it all, and there's no one to tell it to, no
one to trust. Stay close to us, Lord. And help us stay
close to you. Amen.

THE FUNGUS

....
Psalm 73:1-13

Easy answers, I've discovered, are never as easy as they seem. Even when we know what's right, doing it can be tough as nails.

Psalm 73 almost makes me mad. The problem here is envy. The psalmist is talking about how frustrated believers can get when they see really bad people nail down all the raves. Take me, for instance. Sometimes I ask myself why my book doesn't get published when the novels of people who think God is a muskrat, at best, get jubilant reviews from the *New York Times*. Why do bad people have it so good?

You don't have to travel far to understand what the psalm is getting at. The kid with the great '47 Ford truck, fourteen girlfriends, and a couple dozen pairs of designer jeans is also the kid who drinks like a fish and mocks authority. How is it that a real jerk like him has all the friends and all the money while you sit in the corner in your worn-out Levis? That's the question.

It's answered very simply in Psalm 73—look at verses 25 and 26. Wait a minute. Don't. I bet you know the answer already.

Sometimes I think it didn't take world-class talent to write psalms. Anybody can guess the answer to this one: the minute you start wishing you could have all the good things promised in TV commercials, stop. Put your faith in God instead.

That's what I call an easy answer. Sickening.

It's easy because it's so much tougher than it sounds. Of course, sin is a tough problem. I've never killed a soul, never gone out on my wife, never bowed down to any idols. Oh sure, when I was a kid I slicky-slickied a few packs of cigarettes, but that's history. No major sins in my life that I remember.

But sin is more like athlete's foot than a bank heist, I think. I've had athlete's foot since I was a boy. It stinks up your life—and your family's—and it draws monstrously painful cracks between your toes. Sometimes my son checks out the soles of my feet in nauseated awe, the way he checks out industrial-strength centipedes. My feet are that ugly.

Athlete's foot is a fungus that abounds in wet warmth. Just like sin. You can put on ointments and shake on powder; you can wash your feet twice daily, but the fungus is always lurking.

For me at least, it's not hard to avoid killing people or to stay away from other big, bloody sins. But I can't get rid of athlete's foot, that stinking fungus. It's a condition.

Sin is a condition too. It distorts the way we see things just as athlete's foot affects the way I walk. One of the distortions sin creates is envy—our idea that bad people have all the good times. Sin puts strange glasses on our noses, making everything look double-edged.

The problem with Psalm 73 is not that it spits out easy answers, but that the answer is so tough. Fungus sin makes us all limp when we envy others, especially those who don't give two hoots about God. And it's so incredibly hard to fight that kind of sin because it's so much a part of us.

Maybe most of us don't need Christ to keep us from lugging an Uzi into McDonalds and blowing people away. But we can't do without him when it comes to the condition of sin.

He's the world's easiest answer, but that's something you can spend a lifetime learning.

....

Dear Lord, help us to see our own faults rather than training our eyes on the successes and failures of others. All of us wander away, each of us in our own way. Thank you for always bringing us back. Amen.

BABIES HAVING BABIES

....

Psalm 73:2-5

Here are a few statistics from this morning's paper. In the last three years, two out of five women who had their first babies were not married at the time the baby was conceived. Three out of ten weren't married when those babies were born.

Is that alarming? Yes, because the numbers are going up. Ten years ago 33 percent—as compared with 40 percent—were unmarried when they got pregnant; and only 18 percent—not 30 percent— weren't married when the babies were born.

Why are those numbers alarming? I hope you'll believe me when I say that nothing changed my life as much as becoming a father. Parenting—don't let anybody kid you about this—is rough. I shudder, as every serious parent does, when I think about the problem Jesse Jackson called "babies having babies."

Being a mother or a father demands patience, tenderness, love, discipline, toughness. No other job demands so full a range of human capabilities as bringing up a child. It's simply not a job for the immature, whether they're fourteen or forty.

But hold on. Whenever we use the word *pregnant*, we're describing something female. And the danger for men is that they see pregnancy as a woman's problem. According to all the reports I've seen, it still takes two to tango.

One more thing. I don't want to sound "holier than thou." I know lots of good people—Christians—who jumped the gun. Some of them got married; others didn't. Let him or her who is without sin cast the first stone here. Getting pregnant—or getting someone pregnant—is not the mark of Cain.

But how do we explain the fact that more and more illegitimate births occur every year? I think Psalm 73 helps explain some of it, even though this song was written a long time ago.

Cause A: sin. That's the easy answer.

Cause B: abortion and widely available birth-control devices. Methods created to stop unwanted pregnancies seem to make sex safe; yet as the use of these devices becomes more widespread, the number of unwanted pregnancies actually increases. Why? Because making sex "safe" makes love cheap. Why *not* sleep with somebody else? It's not that big a deal.

Cause C: the media. Years ago churches were built in the middle of towns because they stood in the middle of people's lives. Factories changed that. Work became more important than worship. Now factory life, for the most part, is history. We've entered the information age. And today the institution planted in the middle of our lives is—you guessed it—the media.

When is the last time you saw a show about a couple in love deciding to wait to sleep together until they got hitched? I can't remember one. Research shows that 90 percent of the sex on the tube happens outside of marriage. Really.

Psalm 73, as we've noted before, is about envy. The media create our gods—gods who come on stage handsomely, beautifully, dressed in their Guess jeans, here and there just a touch of Calvin Klein's *Obsession*. These beautiful people do it, anytime and all the time. Why shouldn't we?

I only wish it were easier to say with the psalmist here, "My joy lies in being close to God." That's the lesson of Psalm 73.

....

Lord, please bless those kids who are in trouble. Give them strength to hold on to you in the middle of difficult times. Help all of us to keep from stumbling, even when the road is full of gaps and potholes. Thank you for your unfailing love. In Christ's name, Amen.

"GO GET 'EM, SINNERS"

....

Psalm 73:16-28

We all love drawing pictures of God. Some of us think of God as a pipe-smoking, grandfatherly type who smiles down on his children from an oak rocking chair with a lazy comforting squeak. Others want to make that image grandmotherly.

One of the biggest words I know is *anthropomorphism*, a term the dictionary says means "the representation of God with human attributes." We all anthropomorphize.

I don't think the practice of anthropomorphism is really a sin—just a natural outcome of our human limitations. Since we can't really know God fully and completely, our imaginations dress him in human characteristics: if we want a sweet and loving God, we create the grandfather (or grandmother) image. If we want a righteous, judgmental God, we dress him in medieval armor, breastplate, shield, and a sleek Darth Vader helmet.

It appears that God *wants* to be a mystery to us. When Moses nervously accepted God's command to free his people from Egypt, he asked God at least to tell him His name. It didn't seem like such a big request. After all, if God was going to send Moses out to lead a life-threatening revolution, the least God could do would be to let Moses know who He was.

"What am I going to say when people ask me who's behind this whole business?" Moses asked.

And God told him, "I AM." Strange handle. No doubt Moses would have preferred something like "Beauregard the Magnificent."

But what God wanted Moses to know was that He would not be known. He could not be—even by a name—pinned down. God is existence itself. "I AM," he said. He is life.

Even Asaph, in Psalm 73, can't help picture God. And the image he draws, in verse 18, is incredible. The wicked, who look so great, he says to God, are "on a slippery slope. You put them there, and then you urge them on to run."

I love it. God as a cheerleader—or maybe we should say "jeer-leader." Picture this as Asaph does, and it's okay to laugh. A few righteous yuks go nicely with this psalm.

A whole long line of sinful big shots, a whole group of *National Enquirer*'s favorites, trying to keep their balance. But they can't. One after another, they fall, and when they do, they look as bad as I did on my back walk when I cracked a rib.

Zoom!—their feet go up in the air, and they come down on their fannies, bouncing along, hundreds of Charlie Chaplins, spilling into a gaggle of loose arms and legs with a full orchestra of hooting. You know the kind of sound—whhhooooaaaa!!!

And where is God? Asaph says he takes great comfort from the fact that God is there, jeering them on. Picture that if you can. The God of the universe, holding a megaphone, jumping around like a high school cheerleader, urging these sinners to get up and try it again. "Go on," he yells. "Pull yourselves up by your own silly bootstraps." And all the while these wicked fools just keep slipping and sliding, bumping along down toward their ruin.

It would make a wonderful cartoon.

I wouldn't want to try to draw the I AM in a cotton sweater with a varsity letter, but I can't help but laugh to think of it.

To those who love you, Lord, you show love. Thank you for loving us. Forgive us for thinking we are better than others, and stay with us, even in our sin. Thank you for being just. Amen.

SEEING CLEARLY

....
Psalm 73:21-28

Four Roman intellectuals sat around the fountain one day, discussing important matters.

"And what, my friends," Dyspeptic piped, "do you believe to be the best antidote for dimness of vision?"

Scurrilous picked a grape from a nearby bunch. "The question obviously is a trick," he said, "for studies have long shown that nothing clears up vision like smelling salts."

Dubious raised a finger and an eyebrow. "My research concludes," he said, "that eyeglasses are vastly superior."

"Smelling salts!" Scurrilous shouted.

"Eyeglasses!" Dubious maintained.

"Gentlemen!" The sage, Peerless, raised his hands to avoid turning the discussion into a beer commercial. He straightened his toga. "The question is, 'What sharpens the vision?' " His eyes rolled. "And the answer is obvious, my friends: envy—it makes everything look larger."

I'm not sure the punch line is worth the time it took to tell that joke, but I like it anyway.

Envy, tradition has it, is the daughter of pride, borne out of our arrogant sense that we alone are worthy of what others have in their garage. It's self-destructive, since its appetite always craves more, no matter what it's already devoured. Envy destroys us by consuming our hearts and souls.

But it's not just envy that's at the heart of the problem in Psalm 73, although the psalmist admits he almost slipped up by "*envying* the arrogant." What's gnawing at Asaph is an understandable sense of injustice.

It really bugs him, he says, not simply that others have the good he wants, but that those who are blessed are so blasted wicked. Something's rotten in the province when bad people live in Palm Beach mansions and good guys can't afford public housing. That's the problem Asaph struggles with.

The whole psalm is really a testimony. Asaph starts with praise—God is indeed good to Israel. How does Asaph know? From his own experience. I almost stumbled, he confesses. I thought only bad people had it good in the world. Then I figured out the mystery (v. 17).

Asaph says he was wrong to the wicked, that he was blind to the whole truth. When he saw the wicked, they seemed happy. They seemed to be always having a great time. He really believed they had it made.

But once he figured it all out, he saw them fall (v. 19) at God's own urging. Then he knew he hadn't seen them clearly before. Envy, in a way, clouded his vision. Only after he understood God's ways did Asaph realize that well-heeled bozos were much worse off than he was.

The real joy of understanding all of this, Asaph says, is knowing that even when we can't see straight, even when we are green with envy, God still holds on to us. He was there, Asaph says. The bad guys were falling, but God didn't let me slip.

Even in sin, God stays with us. That's the real testimony.

The world according to television seems dazzling, Lord, a Porsche in every garage. Help us not to envy. Help us to stay away from thinking that we'd be a little bit better off with a new car or stereo or designer sweatshirt. Keep us from sin, Lord. In Christ's name, Amen.

PSALM 73

HONESTY VIII

"I'm just glad I never touched that booze," Mike said. "The cops came in at just the right time—ever think of that, Matt?"

He hadn't. He wondered what might have happened if Mike had tanked up on the bottle. Maybe they were supposed to get caught.

The mall was Saturday-afternoon full—too full, Matt thought, too busy to be fun.

"Tell me something," Mike said. "Did you think Whitney was lying when she said she knew the Burger Barn guy? You know her better than I do."

Matt put his hand into the water beneath the fountain. He felt like he had to protect her somehow. "I don't know," he said. "You never know about Whitney."

"You're right about that," Mike said. "I don't know what you see in her. Sometimes she scares me—"

"She does?" Matt said. He shook his arms in front of him.

"She's got the guts of a brass monkey," Mike insisted. "You would never have gone into those apartments—"

"Her dad owns 'em," Matt said.

"You wouldn't have, Matt, and you know it." He pulled the socks up out of his shoes. "Speak of the devil," he said, pointing his head.

It was Whitney with her arms full of bags.

Mike told her all the stuff he'd already told Matt—what his dad had said after they'd left the police station and how surprised he was that Whitney knew the Burger Barn man.

"His name is Elroy," she said.

"Whatever," Mike said and kept right on talking.

Matt kept quiet. He kept wondering about what Mike had said— about Whitney being so tough . . . .

He was still wondering a few minutes later when Mike left him alone with Whitney and headed off toward the arcade.

"How did you know that guy Elroy anyway?" Matt asked when she sat down on the brick beside him. He had to get to the bottom of this.

"Who?"

"The Burger Barn—you know, Elroy? How did you know him?"

"I told you—"

"I know you told us, but nobody thought he'd come down and save our tails. I couldn't believe it."

It wasn't like her to look away the way she did.

"You do something for him, don't you?" he said.

"What do you mean?" she asked.

"How come he seems like he knows you so well, and you never once talked about him before? Something's weird, Whitney," Matt said. "I got to know."

"It's nothing," she said. She looked him straight in the eye. "Sometimes I run errands for him. He says he'll pay me, and it's no big deal. Not all the time. I just deliver stuff—"

"What stuff?—"

"I don't know. I don't open the bags. I'm not supposed to." She was getting mad—he could tell. "Look, Matt, where do you think I got the tapes from? I work. He pays me."

"What's in the bags, Whitney—come on, you know."

"It's not my business."

"You're lying," Matt said.

"What are you thinking?" she asked.

"You know good and well what I'm thinking," he told her. He waited for her to respond, but she turned away. "You know, don't you? You're no dummy, Whitney."

"How am I supposed to know?"

"It's drugs. Don't lie your way out of it."

She shook her blonde hair back from her face and grabbed all her packages. "You're some Christian, buddy boy, accusing me of dealing drugs. You got no proof, do you? Admit it!"

"What's in the bags, Whitney?" Matt asked again.

"I don't know," she insisted, getting to her feet. "But I'm not going to sit here and talk to you anymore—I can tell you that much." When she swung her purse over her shoulder, it nearly hit him. "I don't need you," she said, and walked away, never glancing back.

She was right. She was popular, rich, and good-looking. She didn't need him. But he didn't need her anymore either.

Whitney didn't get lost in the crowd right away because her arms were so full of more clothes, more good stuff for the kid who could already get any guy she wanted.

She didn't even need the Burger Barn guy's money.

He should just let her go, he thought, write her out of his life. He didn't need the kind of junk she was into. He didn't need her. She was like poison, he thought. Better just to get out of her life.

Sometimes the world we live in doesn't make sense, Lord. Help us remember what's easy to say and hard to do—to love you more than anything and to love our neighbors as ourselves. Keep us faithful. Amen.

"HAPPINESS IS . . ."

....

Psalm 84

When a friend of mine visited my college classes last year, he told my students that our particular tribe of Christians—the Reformed tribe—are never very happy.

"When is the last time you remember feeling really, really happy?" he asked the students, pointing at them, one at a time.

Some students couldn't answer. Maybe they didn't dare to remember in public. But other students did have an answer. In both classes, some students said they remembered being really, really happy when their high school basketball teams won tournaments.

The Israelites, of course, never played high school basketball. But Psalms like 84 and 100 are happy psalms—that's obvious.

The Israelites were happy about worship.

Now that fact can make me wrinkle my forehead and sigh deeply, because it makes someone like me, a Reformed Christian, feel guilty. I'm good at that. I know my kids don't always appreciate having to go to church, and I have to admit that there are times I'd rather be waterskiing.

But before we slay ourselves for not being excited about Sunday mornings—or evenings—a couple of things need to be said.

We should remember, first of all, that each psalm carries its own special emotion. We've just looked at a psalm full of envy—Psalm 73. Psalm 51 is a confession. Some psalms, like 13, are whiners. In that one, David says "How long, O Lord" so often that some people have called it "the how-ling psalm."

In Psalms 84 and 100 the emotion is happiness. But we shouldn't conclude that really great believers sit around all hours of the day wishing they were in church. The Israelites didn't—except on special occasions.

That's the second thing we should remember—that both of these psalms are songs to sing on special occasions. Back then, all of God's people were called to gather at Mount Zion, the place where God lived, three times a year. Those gatherings were like festivals. Whole families would pack lunches and take off—for days at a time—to celebrate. In some ways, those festivals were really family and community holidays—like vacations. No wonder these psalms are filled with joy!

Don't conclude from this that carrying a long face around all year is somehow okay as long as you smile two or three days out of the year. If anyone should be happy, Christians should—we're loved like no one else on earth! But nobody can tell me—or you—that YOU MUST BE HAPPY! about church or anything else. That's crazy. Years ago, my mother tried to tell me that I should JUST LOVE! scalloped potatoes. I still won't eat the slimy things.

In the psalms God's people talk honestly to him. Sometimes what they say is wonderful; sometimes it isn't. What's most important, I think, is that they're talking to him, telling him their sorrows and their fears and their joys.

I'm sure all of my students could remember some times in their lives when they were really happy. What's important to them—and God—is that when they are, they tell the Lord about it.

When families don't communicate, they break down. It's no different in the family of God.

Dear Lord, our happiness comes from you. The great moments of our lives, the best days, the sweetest afternoons, and the most fun-filled nights all belong to you. Keep us in touch with your grace in everything we do, always. Amen.

A JOYFUL NOISE

....

Psalm 100

Nobody still drawing breath on this earth has more than a hint of an idea of what we'll be doing in heaven. My daughter would be happy, I think, simply if her friends were there; and my son would like it as long as the place offered an arcade. Skateboarders would want rinks; surfers, waves; hunters, woods; cooks, kitchens; and politicians, hands to shake.

It's not "in" today to think of heavenly choirs, even though Christians for centuries have pictured themselves decked out in white robes and standing, like a haloed Mormon Tabernacle Choir, on heavenly risers. People today say that singing an endless medley of hymns doesn't really appeal to them. "If heaven is like junior choir," some kids wonder, "do we have options?"

I, for one, think we could do worse than singing.

Now I'm no musician. I was a horrible failure at trumpet; I took piano for umpteen years, and today I can't even play a hymn. I can number the choirs I sang with on one hand. But I'd still hold out for one huge choir up there, millions of glad voices, even if we've got a couple hundred thousand people who can't hold a tune in a flat catcher's mitt built for knuckleballs.

Last night we had a community worship service in the big chapel here in town, and the place was packed—a couple thousand people, at least. I may be strange, but whenever I sing hymns I love in a huge body of believers, I have to stop. Some silly emotion jerks at every muscle of my face—my eyes tear, my lips quiver, and finally my voice simply shuts down. It's embarrassing.

I remember very well the first time that ever happened to me. I was a seventh grader at a statewide music festival for Christian school kids in Waupun, Wisconsin—one of two hundred kids on gym bleachers, all singing "Jesu, Joy of Man's Desiring."

Now I was as macho as any big-time seventh-grade boy, and the only real reason I had looked forward to going halfway across the state was to be with the girls. But there I was, in the middle of the bleacher pack, choking back tears. It was frightening. Someone could have seen me. All I knew was that what was making me shake had something to do with beauty—of all things!—something I had always thought *real* boys didn't buy into. That's why I didn't tell a soul.

But there was something about all of us singing that song that stopped me in my tracks. Its lilting reverence flowed in a litany of arpeggios, something never-ending, through chords that seemed almost to meditate. Of course, I couldn't analyze it then, but I knew I felt something really beautiful.

Maybe it's for that same reason that I've always liked Psalm 100, especially in the old King James Version: "Make a joyful noise unto the Lord, all ye lands; serve the Lord with gladness, come before his presence with singing." Of course, that psalm isn't just *my* favorite. I'm sure others claim it too.

To me, there's nothing quite as beautiful as a huge crowd of believers singing praises together, and that's why, I guess, as old-fashioned as it sounds, I rather like the idea of heaven itself as one beautiful unending song.

When we have it good, Lord, it's almost hard to think
of heaven. But help us not to forget that whatever
joys we feel on earth are nothing compared to what
we will experience when we live forever in your front
yard. We thank you for loving us so much. In Jesus'
name, Amen.

THE RIGHTEOUS FALL

....

Psalm 84:4-5

Years ago in the town where I grew up, a preacher left his wife and family and took off with another woman from the church. The whole town wept over what had happened, both those who were members of this preacher's church and those who weren't.

His case probably wasn't the only incident of adultery in town that year, but because this man was a preacher, most people sat around in gloom, wondering about the state of the world.

It's not hard to understand why. We don't *expect* regular people to take off on their spouses or drink too much booze or abuse their children. When it happens, we shake our heads and wince. Yet we know things like that happen.

But we *never* expect that kind of junk from our preachers—maybe because we don't think of them as "regular people," even though they are.

Neither, apparently, did the person who wrote Psalm 84. "Blessed are those who dwell in your house; they are ever praising you," he says in verse 4. It seems the writer figured that a lifetime spent in the heavenly temple could, single-handedly, clean people from the inside out.

The Israelites' great temple was not quite the same as the brick church down the block, of course. Old Testament Jews felt God actually lived in the temple—and only there. No Christian I know makes that claim for his or her church today.

But even back then, temple dwellers—the priests and the Levites— were not perfect human beings. Eli was a terrible father, if you remember; and Aaron, like Korah after him, had a freeway-wide streak of envy right through his vision.

The fact of the matter is, nobody's perfect—not even Mother Teresa or Billy Graham. And it's my guess that those two would be the first to admit it.

So is the psalmist wrong?

Not really. Look at what he says in verse 5: "Blessed are those whose strength is in you, who have set their hearts on pilgrimage." It really makes no difference if those who invest their strength in God are preachers or masons or librarians, whether they spend their waking hours in an office or a kitchen or a classroom. Where they live isn't important. Where they put their trust is.

One of the great truths of the Reformation is something called "the priesthood of all believers." What that means, quite simply, is that all of God's children—not just those who hang around in monasteries or brick churches—are holy.

What makes us—and our work—holy is not what we do. We're not saved by keeping our soybean fields weedless or by refraining from shouting at sales clerks. I won't be saved by writing another ten thousand of these little meditations. We don't earn life with Christ.

What makes all of us holy—even the preachers who fall—is God's gift of love. It's Christ whose life brings forgiveness.

By the way, today that preacher I was talking about—he's back in the pulpit. He knows about gifts, I'm sure.

Bless all of our work, Lord, whether it's done with a
Farmall tractor or an Apple computer or a dustmop.
May everything we do bring you praise. Amen.

PILGRIMAGE

....

Psalm 100

There would be no stopping them now, Hamak thought. He glanced at his sandals and laughed to remember how not four days earlier he'd thought they would never make it to Jerusalem—neither he nor his sandals nor his family.

They'd started out with only a few other families. He and his parents and brothers and sisters had taken up their bundles and marched slowly through the passes, next to boulders as big as the wheels on their wagon. But after just two days on the road, the wagon's axle had broken, and Hamak had wondered if all the planning, all the preparation, had been in vain. Neither of his parents had doubted, but Hamak had looked at the broken axle, at the wagon jammed awkwardly against the rocks, and had started to think that they would never make it to the celebration this year.

But as the day passed, many others came—a dozen, then fifty, then hundreds, following on the valley road, men and women and children beyond number. When some of these strangers had hoisted the wagon off the ground, Hamak felt as if he'd seen a miracle.

"Nothing will stop this wagon," his father had said, pulling a fist together and raising it. "We are God's people going to worship him, the God of Israel."

And the others, strong men he'd never seen before, raised their hands with his father and started in singing a song he'd known himself since he was a child: "My soul longeth, yea, even fainteth for the courts of the Lord; my heart and my flesh crieth out for the living God."

Hamak had never heard anything quite like it. All down the dusty road behind them, people sang along as the music swelled to their ears. Their joyous singing was like water in the desert sun.

At night the lights of campfires danced over the land like a million candles. As Hamak lay back against the night and waited for sleep, his family beside him, he heard echoes here and there of more songs of Zion.

Every mile closer to Jerusalem, from every village gate and every city wall, more of God's people joined the march until the processional flowed out in joy behind them like a river of life. When Hamak's family had been alone, the long trip had seemed impossible. But now, with so many of God's people, how could they not make it? Wherever Hamak looked, he could see parents and children, laughing and singing with the chorus of thousands, their sweet voices cheerful and joyous. It was as if the world's every soul had thrown down their nets, their hoes, all their tools, and joined in the praise of the great God, the Creator, the I AM who'd taken them out of the wilderness and freed them from Egyptian slavery.

Hamak knew he would never forget the pilgrimage of thousands to the house of the Lord. The songs of God would play forever in his mind and heart.

Bring us to your church with joy in our hearts, even when we'd rather be somewhere else. Don't let us forget how good it is to live in the presence of your chosen people, men and women who love and serve you. In Christ's name, Amen.

HONESTY IX

"So what's happening with Bonnie and Clyde?" Adkins said on Tuesday after class. He'd grabbed Matt's shoulder on his way out and sort of nodded to let him know that he wanted to talk. "You got her thrown in jail yet?" he asked.

Matt dropped his books on a desk. "It's all over," he said. "No sweat. It's not my problem anymore."

"Is that right?" Adkins said. He stuck a red pencil in the sharpener and turned it, making a sound through his lips like a motorcycle. "You wrote her off, huh?" he said. He blew on the point when he took it out. "You let her have it." He poked the pencil at an imaginary balloon, then pretended it exploded.

"I don't need her," Matt said. "She's in deep trouble, deeper than I thought. I quit her."

"Good," Adkins said, "you deserve a medal. Just dropping people when they're in trouble—that takes guts." He stuck the pencil between his fingers and rapped his hand hard on the table, breaking the pencil cleanly.

"What'd you do that for?" Matt said.

"Ah, I don't need it anymore," Adkins said. "May as well forget it." He tossed the two ends in the basket and went back to his desk. "See ya'," he said.

"Well, big help you are," Matt said.

"You don't need help," Adkins said. "You know how to live. When somebody's in trouble, you just quit, break 'em in half—and you come out smelling like a rose."

"She doesn't need me," Matt insisted. "She as much as told me that. She's in big-time trouble, but she walked away from me."

Adkins took his coat off the back of his chair and pulled it over his shoulders. "Tell you what, Matt, why don't you just stop off at the washroom on your way out and wash your hands good."

"I don't get it," Matt said.

Adkins reached down into the wastebasket and picked out the broken red pencil, then held it up in his hands. "This isn't worthless, you know—even though it's broken," he said. "And you can't just walk away from someone who's in trouble—you hear me? If that was the way things were supposed to be, Christ would have never come down here for you and me, would he?—"

"I don't get it," Matt said.

"Think about it," Adkins told him. "I'm going home." He circled the desk and came down the row where Matt was standing. "Here, sharpen these for me, will you?" he said, dropping the pencil pieces right in front of Matt.

"Listen," Matt said, "I can't do miracles."

Adkins stopped right at the door and looked around. "No?" he said. "Then maybe you're right. Why don't you go hide somewhere. Maybe it'll all go away."

"What do you want me to do?" Matt asked.

"What's changed?" Adkins answered. "I want you to pray. Tell God everything. You been doing that?"

"Sure," Matt said, but he knew it was a lie.

"Then you'll know what to do."

Matt nodded.

"Chapters four and five," Adkins said, pointing at his math book, "test tomorrow." And then he just walked away.

Down the hall Matt heard the cheerleaders going through their routines. He looked at his watch and figured he was already late for his paper route. Outside the window, the sky was a heavy, dismal gray.

Matt knew he shouldn't just give up on Whitney. That was just the easy way out. He ought to try at least. If no one stopped her, she was going to get in much deeper than she had ever imagined.

But what could he do? He was only a kid, and besides, she'd taken off on him, walked away into the crowd, leaving him sitting there at the fountain in the mall. She didn't even want him in her life. How was he supposed to say anything now?

Nobody could do a thing, nobody at all, probably not even her parents. Nobody could touch her anymore. Nobody.

Except maybe God.

God made her, he thought, and He can put her back together. It isn't like Humpty-Dumpty really, he thought, because you can take a pencil broken right in half and still make it write.

Ever since Whitney had walked off, Matt had told himself there was nothing he could do. But maybe he was wrong.

"I don't know what I can do for Whitney," he told God, right there in the math room, "but if there *is* something I can do, help me to find out what it is." He didn't even close his eyes. "You made her—now help her too. And if you want, you can use me. I'll try my best."

Then he sharpened all three ends of the broken red pencil and left both pieces on Adkin's desk. He left a note too—"Don't use these on my papers, buddy"—and signed his initials.

....

When it's hard to do what's right, Lord, give us the strength and assurance that you will stay with us, no matter what comes down the road. Keep us in touch. Amen.

ANGER

....

Psalm 7

Let's just fool around here for a minute. I'll give you five situations. You tell me which of them would make you the most angry.

Situation #1: You're at a track meet, a big one, standing around with maybe twenty kids, waiting for the 800 meters. You recognize the hot-shot runner from East—the one with the Flo-Jo fingernails. You hear her say, "Central [your school] is such a dump—kids from there are so gross—"

Situation #2: Somewhere in the Middle East a gang of thugs take foreign hostages. A Moslem crowd goes mad, screaming about the satanic United States (or Canada). They haul out a blindfolded hostage from your country and hit him. The crowd loves it. You see it all on television.

Situation #3: You're minding your own business, riding your bike along a quiet city street, when this kid you don't even know whistles, then makes an obscene gesture at you. The very moment you look at him, you smack right into a pickup truck.

Situation #4: You see pictures of starving people in Africa—kids with distended bellies and buzzing flies around their eyes, mothers with matchstick bones. When you read the article, you find out that their government does nothing to help them.

Situation #5: A girl in your class is crying in school. She claims her dad lost his job, and now they have to move. You feel sorry for her, even though you don't know her very well; but when you go up to her, she gets hot. She says your dad is at fault because he's the banker that wouldn't give them a loan. Then she calls your father a name I won't repeat. You love your father.

Which of these five situations makes you boil? Which of them makes you hiss? Which one makes you want to scream?

If any one emotion characterizes Psalms 7 and Psalm 137—it's anger. In both, the psalmists raise their fists like madmen. (Isn't it strange that we can use the word *mad* to mean "insane," as well as "angry"?)

But isn't anger really sin?

No. Take Jody. Her mother is in the hospital for drinking too much. Jody's home, taking care of her little brothers. She loves her mother, but when she finds a bottle hidden in a bedroom closet she flies into a rage. She hates liquor with a passion.

We can get angry about sin all we want and not sin for a moment in doing it.

The problem is that all too often what angers us is not sin, but what hurts us personally. We get most upset about things that injure us. I admit it—running into the back of that pickup would make me scream. I'd be hot. Starving people in Timbuktu would make me feel more sad than angry, but I wouldn't hiss at those pictures like I would at the kid down the street.

I may be wrong, but I'd guess most of you are like me. We get angry at things that affect us personally, that injure our own pride. That kind of anger is sin. My guess is that your list would read something like this: 3, 5, 1, 2, 4. Look at the list: the situations become progressively less and less personal.

Anger itself isn't evil. Christ didn't tiptoe around the money changers. There's a lot of sin in this world—a lot to get angry about. Just don't use anger to protect your own turf.

....

Give us the ability to see when it's okay to be angry,
Lord. Help us to know when it's not just ourselves
we're protecting. Stay with us, Lord, all the time. In
your Son's name, Amen.

BROKEN-BONE BLESSINGS

....
Psalm 7:9-13

Not long ago two young men, one at a time, sat on hard metal chairs before a church consistory to profess their faith— something some people call "joining the church." Actually, both of them had long ago been members of God's family.

One of the two, a big college kid, claimed that studying biology helped him to see God even in the world of microscopic beings most of us never see. The other, still in high school, said he'd come simply because he was ready to tell people about his faith, something he'd felt already for a long time.

Consistory meetings can be boring—too much bickering and complaining, much of it over stuff that goes on month after month. Nothing lights up a consistory like kids professing their faith. That night, at least for an hour, the whole room glowed in the Spirit-warmed profession of two young men who talked openly about themselves and their God.

When the two were asked about big moments in their lives, they said the same thing. They were both injured in motorcycle accidents, and both of them admitted, their lips quivering a little, that while they were lying in hospital beds they'd come much closer to understanding who they were—and who God is.

It might seem strange that bad accidents were good moments in their lives. I'm sure the accidents weren't big thrills to their moms and dads. Yet, being laid up that way taught both young men something about death, they said—and life. Their broken bones, it seems, became a blessing.

There's a passage in the book of Romans from which many, many generations of Christians have taken great comfort. Maybe you know it: "In all things God works for the good of those who love him, who have been called according to his purpose." It's a strange thing how God sometimes wrestles our problems into blessings.

David confesses in verse 11 of Psalm 7 that God the judge dispenses wrath as well as blessing every day. This picture of David's God isn't cute, like some Precious Moments knick-knack. The very idea of God Almighty slinging fiery arrows at the world isn't something you want to run right out and tell your friends about. After all, who'd want a part of that God?

Is David right, or is he just ornery? We may not like to admit it, but he's probably right. God *does* beam out anger every day—sometimes, I suppose, in the form of motorcycle accidents. I'm not saying that God actually caused the accidents these guys suffered. However, bad things happen. We all know that.

But look at verse 10. According to David, God shields those who are "upright in heart."

Does that mean that Christians never get banged up? No. However, it helps explain how God can turn even what seem to be bad things into life-changing moments.

I wish I knew who said this, but I don't. It's just one of those little lines that's worth repeating. "God doesn't save his people *from* bad storms; he saves them *in* bad storms."

Nobody likes motorcycle accidents. But God has a way of turning darkness into light, because in all things he works for the good of those who love him. Believe me, truth is sometimes hard to take, but that doesn't make it any less the truth.

Dear Lord, when the world really gets dark, help us
to remember that you'll always be with us. Amen.

SUPPING WITH THE DEVIL

....

Psalm 7:14-17

The old saying goes, "He who sups with the Devil had best use a long spoon."

The Psalm says something similar: "The guy who digs holes sometimes falls in."

Gregg's mom says his Aunt Gracie is a pack rat who simply can't throw anything away. "Her attic is full of junk," she says to her husband one night at the table. "I don't know how she'll ever move to that little apartment."

Gregg's got a nose for possibilities. Aunt Gracie's only son, Harold, is forty, at least, and if Harold was at all normal as a kid, he probably had baseball cards. So Gregg goes to visit Aunt Gracie, sits through horribly dry cake and warm milk, then pops the question: "Did Harold ever have baseball cards?" he asks, with a cute little grin.

Aunt Gracie takes Gregg up to her legendary attic and points him at a pile of shoe boxes. There are hundreds of them—Henry Aarons, Al Kalines, Yogi Berra's rookie year.

"I like old cards," Gregg says, like a sweet little kid. "You think I could take a few home?"

Aunt Gracie's soft as summer fudge. "Sure," she says. "Harold doesn't even know I have them."

He grabs a $100 Mickey Mantle, a Whitey Ford, and a Ted Williams. "Just a few," he says. "Old ones are kind of neat."

When he shows his friends, their eyes bulge. "Incredible," they say. "You just pick these up for nothing?"

But Gregg can't let well enough alone. He figures getting the first three was easy. If he could sit through a little more stale cake and warm milk, he'd have a treasure. Beats buying.

Aunt Gracie's dumb as tar. "Your mother's been telling me for years that I ought to get rid of some of this stuff. Go ahead and take some more."

He grabs a stack three-inches thick. An Eddie Matthews from 1957, the year the Braves won the pennant. A couple of Warren Spahns, three—count 'em, three!—Roger Maris cards, including a '61.

Gregg's got it made. His buddies flock around to see the cards. He says he's got this rich aunt, and he laughs like mad.

One Saturday Gregg and his family come home and find the house broken into. "I can't believe it," his dad tells the insurance man. "Some guy breaks into this place, leaves the stereo and the TV, and takes Gregg's cards. Makes no sense."

"Any of his cards worth anything?" the guy asks.

Gregg can't say a thing because he lied to Aunt Gracie. "Nawww," he says. But inside, he's bawling his eyes out.

A week later Aunt Gracie calls and talks to Gregg's dad. "The strangest thing happened," she says. "My Harold called from New York. He says he wants his cards. I gave some of them to Gregg," she tells his father. "Quite a few too. Can you believe my Harold wants them? Could you have Gregg bring them back? Who ever would have thought anybody would want old baseball cards?"

Gregg's dad is right outside his room, coming for the cards. Gregg's inside, listening to tapes. He feels sick about losing all those cards—hundreds of dollars, maybe more. He had them in his hands, for pity's sake. They were his. Maris, Mantle.

"Gregg," his dad says, "that was Aunt Gracie."

"He who sups with the Devil had best use a long spoon."

··

Nobody's perfect, Lord, but we still have to keep
working at it. When we fail, keep us from going
down hard. Forgive us, Lord, for all of our sins.
Amen.

A FRIEND YOU CAN TRUST

....
Psalm 137

In case you've missed it so far, one of the ideas that we've been over time and time again is how the psalmists speak honestly to God. That's because this business of honesty is important. When the psalmists talk to God, they speak to him as if he were beside them, listening constantly—always there, ready.

My wife says a friend is someone you can trust with your deepest feelings, someone you know will listen and never whisper a word to anyone else. A friend is someone to whom you can pour out your soul. God is a trusted friend to the psalmists.

For the defeated people of Israel—a people wiped out by the Babylonians, forcibly evicted from their homes, forced to watch family and friends tortured and killed—a desire for vengeance was understandable. But, as we discover in Psalm 137, they took even their vengeance to God, honestly.

"O Daughter of Babylon, doomed to destruction, happy is he who repays you for what you have done to us—he who seizes your infants and dashes them against the rocks."

No line in the psalms seems quite as painful and honest as that line. These people—the few who survived—had suffered beyond anything I've ever known. Their towns were burned, their lives destroyed, their God wretchedly mocked.

And then, as if to heap on the horror, the Babylonians asked them to sing the songs of Zion for their damned entertainment. The murderers wanted to dance in their own bloody glory. "Play for us," they screamed, their swords pointed at the necks of the vanquished. "Make us happy."

Inside, the Jews pleaded for God's vengeance. That's the record of Psalm 137.

If you had been a Polish Jew in 1944, someone running from death itself, and if you had hidden along the railroad tracks in the forests between Tarnow and Belzec, you would have found among the stones and weeds dozens of photographs of Jewish families, pictures scribbled full of pleas for help. You would have known that those pictures of your own people had been thrown from the death train, wooden boxcars rammed full of human beings bound, like cattle, for death in concentration camps like Bergen Belsen or Auschwitz.

Imagine yourself picking one up. A man stands with his family, smiles on all of their faces. They're dressed in their best, and the tiniest daughter—her hair tied up with bow—is looking at her mother, not the camera. Mom can't help but smile.

On the back, only two words in Yiddish—"Help, please."

Imagine that these are your people. The day you stand there, you know that that family is quite likely dead—shot maybe, or gassed, even the little girl. You wonder about life's worth.

If you talk to God with that picture still in your fingers, just one of dozens at your feet, you will likely say exactly what the exiled Jews said thousands of years before, their harps hung from the trees, their eyes full of tears.

They were honest. They talked to God.

Be with those who really suffer, Lord. Help us to know who they are, and give us strength to help in your name. Amen.

PSALMS 7 & 137

HONESTY X

The papers on Thursday were super light, so Matt finished his deliveries early and headed over to the Pop Shop at the mall for something to drink. Armond, the crazy janitor, was emptying bins around the cafeteria. He had his hair in a ponytail, as usual.

"Hey, Matt-chew," Armond said, in the way he always said it. He knew all the guys because they hung around so often. Armond was a little slow in the head, and sometimes kids made fun of him. "Shopping?" he asked.

"Stopped in for something to drink," Matt said.

"Thirsty, eh?" he asked.

It was like Armond always to say the obvious. That's what made him funny.

He lifted the inside bin out of a trash container and emptied it into his big plastic truck. "I seen the girls," he said almost triumphantly. "I seen Whitney just awhile ago. She's pretty. She's your girl, isn't she, Matt-chew?" Then he giggled. "She's with her brother, I think."

"What'd the guy look like?" Matt asked.

"Just a regular guy—older guy, you know?"

It had to be the Burger Barn creep. Whitney had no older brother. Matt looked at his watch. Maybe he should just walk through the mall and try to find her, he thought. "Thanks, Armond," he said. "You're a buddy, you know that?"

Armond beamed. "Sure," he said.

Matt saw her in a gift shop, the kind with all the gag junk and the dirty books. She was looking at jewelry. Some clerk in a pink apron showed her necklaces off the rack behind her.

Adkins had said not to give up, but there was no way that Matt could just walk in that store and lay it on her, tell her she was getting herself in big trouble. He couldn't. So he sat on the bench outside and watched the clerk lay gold necklaces, one after another, over her head, four or five at least.

Her dad was rich and could afford that stuff, he told himself. Besides, it wasn't like Whitney was in some high-class jewelry store or anything. It was only Diamond's Gifts, the place his parents had kept him out of when he was a kid. So the necklaces didn't mean she was in trouble. Maybe he was overreacting.

Whitney was pretty all right. Armond wasn't wrong about that. She reached back around her head and unclasped the necklaces, one after other, each time checking the mirror on the counter, turning her head to see what she liked. Pretty.

When Whitney had them all off, the clerk laid the gold strands each over her hand and headed for the register. Whitney tossed her hair back and followed the clerk toward the front of the store.

That's when Matt saw the Burger Barn man, the guy she called Elroy. He came up from the back by the posters and the black lights, this sappy smile on his face.

The clerk punched in the prices one at a time, then wrapped each of the necklaces in tissue paper. Elroy reached for his billfold, took out some bills, and gave them to the clerk. Whitney pointed at one of the necklaces, and the clerk unwrapped it. Elroy grabbed it and laid it very gently around Whitney's neck, like some sugar-daddy, then took the scissors from the clerk and snipped off the sales tag, looked at Whitney for what seemed forever with this big leering smile. When Whitney put her arms around him and hugged him, one of her feet came off the floor.

Matt didn't know why exactly, but he felt like bawling. He could feel anger flowing through his body. It shook his fingers, grabbed at his breath, and ran like heat through his arms. He wanted to quit, right then and there. He wanted to tell Adkins that she just wasn't worth it, not when she took money from that scumball.

When they left the store, Matt sat on the opposite side of the bench, leaning down on his elbows so they wouldn't see him. All he could do was tremble. He remembered what Adkins had said about being honest to God, but he was afraid that what he'd say would turn into flames. "Get her away from that bugger," he said. "Please God, he'll drag her somewhere horrible."

Still boiling, he ran into Mike just outside the entrance.

"We got to do something about Whitney, Mike," he said. "I mean it. She's going down bad."

"What do you care?" Mike said. "Let her go."

"I care," he said. "I can't just let her down."

Mike didn't say a thing at first. He just looked at Matt as if there were something he didn't understand. "What you got in mind?" he said. "Let's hear it."

....

When our friends really fail us, don't let us get super-righteous about things. Help us know when and how to help. Direct our lives to do your will. In Jesus' name, Amen.

OLD GLOOMY BROWN

....

Psalm 77

I wish we had room in this meditation for "Young Goodman Brown," a story by Nathaniel Hawthorne, but we don't. Chances are, someday you'll have to read that story. For now, all I can do is tell you a little about it.

"Young Goodman Brown" is about a young Puritan in New England who knows it's time for him to go out into the dark woods to have a look at the world's ugliness. When he does, he meets up with a man who resembles his father but carries a cudgel and acts very much like Satan in disguise. This so-called guide leads him down a dark path where he sees his Sunday School teacher fooling around with the Devil. He can't believe it. He blinks and blinks, but she's still there, this woman he'd always respected.

That's not the end. His cloven-hoofed buddy next shows him the village preacher on his way to a rendezvous with a crowd of devil-worshipers. "My goodness," Young Goodman Brown thinks, "is everyone full of sin? Even the preacher!—"

Deeper and deeper they push into the darkness, until they reach the coven fires burning through the gloom. Young Goodman is speechless, because the place is jammed with people he's respected, people he thought were really, really good, all of them romping around the campfire, dancing like demons.

But what shocks him is that his own wife, Faith, is there. He tries to shout at her, to warn her, and when he does he seems to awaken from a dream.

But he doesn't forget what he's seen. Hawthorne ends the story by saying how Mr. Brown—who is no longer young, or even very good for that matter—dies, years later, in the deepest, darkest gloom. Doubt killed his spirit, made him suspicious of everyone, turned his joy into darkness. Not even in death—not even by escaping the ugliness—could he find any happiness.

Hawthorne's story is one of the most famous tales in American literature because it so vividly reflects what all people go through when they first see real ugliness. That vision of evil threatens to poison our lives and make us suspicious, sour-faced old hammerheads, like Old Man Brown.

I once had a student who found out that one of her junior high teachers—a Christian, a teacher she just loved—had become a homosexual and had stopped believing in God. My student cried and cried, unable at first to accept the reality of evil in her world.

Sometimes, like Goodman Brown, people *never* really recover from such revelations. Things like that murder their souls.

Psalm 77 is all about Goodman Brown's problem—about doubt. "Is God really gone?" the psalmist asks in verse 8. "Is all that good stuff he promised no more than hot air? Maybe he's just forgotten how to love. Maybe God's on vacation."

Those words seem horribly cruel. But sometimes people—good people—feel that way.

Young Goodman Brown knew that he *had* to go into the woods. All of us do. Everyone feels horribly let down by God at some time in life. If you haven't yet, you probably will.

When you do, remember Psalm 77. Just keep talking to God. Tell him everything. The psalmist doubts, but he doesn't lose God—and God never loses him.

....

In times of doubt, help us to keep talking to you,
Lord. You are our Rock, even when we're afraid
we've been left alone and helpless. In Christ's name,
Amen.

LEAVING THE NEST

....

Psalm 77:1-9

The swallows in our garage are great parents, and I love them—even if they always dirty our car.

Okay, I admit it, I'm a softie when it comes to this little swallow family, and I have been for the last several years. When they come back, I just can't chase them away. Half the time I park the car outside in the sun just to avoid bombardment.

I especially love to watch the swallows fly. Jays lumber through the air, finches lilt, and robins bob. But swallows slice; they veer expertly. Besides, they're cute. Beneath their matching Batman capes, Mom is yellow and Dad is orange.

It's been dry here recently, but last Saturday we had an inch of rain that fell so nicely, half the town was out to watch it. I stood inside our garage and watched the drops flatten against the pavement and turn the lawn emerald.

Mom Swallow didn't like me standing there. She'd flit out to the end of the driveway, zoom back toward me, flip at the last possible moment, veering off. I was standing between her and the kids.

I wondered how long she could take the extra burden of the rain. She can't weigh more than an ounce. But she kept coming at me, as if she could throw fear into the heart of a man whose beard likely outweighs her.

Finally I got out of her way, and she flew back in to her children.

Today my kids hit tennis balls up against the garage door. Once they quit, I saw Mom Swallow sit on the cement in front of the door and wiggle in through a crack. She had to feed the chicks, door or no door.

Every summer a new brood of baby swallows have to learn to get out on their own. It must be great to be loved as they are. They can't *want* to leave the nest.

But they have to. That's life in the big city.

The only world they know is the big dipper of dried mud that Mom and Dad spit together for a nest against a rafter. I've never looked inside, but I bet it's soft, insulated with a quilt of feathers. But the time comes when the young sparrows have to leave their childhood behind and find their own way.

Christian parents—like most parents, I suppose—worry about their children leaving the nest—even though kids, like birds, have to. Parents worry because part of growing up is shucking off some things that aren't your own. Christian parents worry that their kids will shuck off faith—that when they leave the nest, they'll leave Christ behind in the feathers.

Some of us have already left the nest. The rest of you will have to someday—perhaps someday soon. Kids aren't clones. You'll choose how you want to live. You'll question whether you need God. You may well doubt that God is really around—just as the psalmist does.

Christian parents hope that when their kids leave the nest, they'll pack faith in their souls. I know. I'm one of those parents.

Thank you for our Christian parents, Lord, but give us our own faith. We know that it's something we must take for ourselves someday. Help us to see our way through a world of our own. Amen.

MEMORIES OF MIRACLES

....
Psalm 77:10-20

When the United States Army's 102nd Infantry Division liberated Gardelegen, Poland, on April 16, 1945, they found more than one thousand burned bodies. The commander of that batallion was so outraged that he ordered the German civilians to build individual six-foot by three-foot coffins for each of the dead.

The report from that day reads this way: "The Second Batallion . . . discovered near Gardelegen an atrocity so awful that it might well have been committed in another era, or indeed on another planet." We can only wish that it had.

What happened? Early in 1945, the Nazis knew they were running out of time. The war would soon be over. The Russian army was already racing in from the east, and the Americans were pressing ever closer from the west.

In addition to taking care of themselves, the Nazis had to do something to get rid of their prisoners, especially the many they called undesirables—including hundreds of thousands of European Jews.

Time, out of their control, pushed them to dispose of those prisoners in the fastest and most economical way possible. Just outside of Gardelegen, they found an old stone barn full of straw. After dousing it well with kerosene, they shoved more than one thousand men in, locked the door, and set the place ablaze.

One eyewitness remembers the shouts—and especially the prayers—that rose from that barn as flames twisted up from its roof and windows. She says that several different languages combined to ask for the same miracle: "Oh God, save us." Even when many of the voices were silent, others kept praying, shouting for God's help.

Suddenly, the sky went dark as night. Lightning danced in unfurled yellow ribbons through black skies, and thunder pounded down. The rain came in sheets—so much, so fast, that the burning barn was doused by the storm.

Miraculously, a handful of young men walked out of that barn and away from certain death.

The next day, the Americans found 1016 bodies in what was left of the place. But those who survived—Jews and Gentiles, Americans, Czechs, and Poles—knew that God himself had saved them by his righteous heavenly surf.

Even though most of the people herded into that barn died, I call what happened that day in Poland something of a miracle.

I need those stories. I think we all do. My guess is that if you would ask your own grandparents about "miracles" in their lives, most of them might even remember a time or two when something totally unforeseen happened to keep danger away.

Psalm 77 is something like the story of a fiery barn at Gardelegen, Poland, in 1945. It starts in horror, ends in grace. What the psalmist says almost seems horrible. He thinks God has forgotten him. He wonders whether God has simply chosen to break his promises of love or if he's just run out of mercy.

But then, he says, "I will remember the deeds of the Lord; yes, I will remember your miracles of long ago." When he does, those memories of miracles bring him back to faith.

Like the psalmist, we all need to remember our Gardelegens.

Dear Lord, sometimes when we read the news of history, we can't quite believe what kind of horror people are capable of. Help us to remember the miracles too. Give us strength through great stories of faith. Amen.

WELCOME TO MY NIGHTMARE

....
Psalm 77

I like my dentist, but I hate going there. I always have. I have extra-sensitive teeth—either that or I'm a chicken.

The first time I took my daughter to the dentist, I thought she was much too young to have to suffer. But I took her, and she had a little baby tooth filled. When it was over, this dark-haired dentist, a tall man who really knows how to talk to little kids, told Andrea that she couldn't just shovel in the candy anymore. Candy, he said, would make more cavities—and that day she knew for sure what a cavity was.

I felt sorry for Andrea because candy was just about all she ever dreamed of at that age. She'd learned, sitting there in the chair, that an ugly witch named Tooth Decay lived in the candy house. From that day on, gremlins would live in every peanut butter kiss.

That day was almost like an introduction to sin for her.

But what the psalmist feels in Psalm 77 is tougher and deeper than knowing that you can't have a Three Musketeers whenever you're hungry. Remember Jerelyn Comisky, the girl whose parents split up? Jerelyn's experience comes a whole lot closer to the hurt the psalmist feels.

Jerelyn's mother works at an electronics store all day, then cleans offices at night, late, after the little girls are in bed. She's got two jobs because one check didn't stretch far enough to keep food on the table and clothes on the kids' backs.

At supper, her hair is matted and lifeless. She's worn the same clothes for months, and everything is starting to look dreary. Often, she doesn't have time for any makeup. She's put on weight around the hips, and her short-sleeve dresses fit too tightly around the arms. "She used to be so pretty," Jerelyn thinks helplessly.

When her mother leaves, Jerelyn puts the girls to bed. They don't always listen. "You're not my boss," Ginger tells her. "You can't always tell me what to do."

One night, after her sisters are in bed, Jerelyn discovers they have no clean clothes for school. She hauls two hampers into the basement and does a huge wash.

Then she remembers the dishes. She walks over to the sink and sees dozens of honey ants running around the gravy left on the plates. Her supper almost comes up. She snaps on the light above the sink, and the bulb blows. Just then Ginger comes down and announces that Paula has been sick, right in her bed.

Jerelyn feels helpless, angry, hurt, frightened. Her mother is gone; she hasn't heard from her dad since he left. And there she stands—ten o'clock at night, both girls awake, with a notebook of homework to do before morning.

It's not hard for Jerelyn to hate her father, and it's not hard for her to wonder whether the God she was brought up to believe in has simply forgotten their family. It's not hard for her to think that all of that junk her parents used to say about minding God's Word is just so much Dream Whip.

Jerelyn needs to read Psalm 77. She needs to be reminded that God hasn't forgotten to love her—that he wants her to talk to him and tell him all of her hurt and frustration. Yes, even her doubts.

....

Lord, bless the Jerelyns of this world. Be with those kids and grown-ups who feel as if there's no way to the end of the road. Help them not to despair. Stay close beside them like the friend you are. In Jesus' name, Amen.

PSALM 77

HONESTY XI

Adkins was dressed to kill. The grease he used to slick back his hair shone like silver in the darkness. He had picked up a mustache some-place, and wore this fancy trench coat over his shirt and tie.

It wasn't hard to recruit him. Matt and Mike had gone in after school and told him their plan, how they needed somebody—an adult—to scare the dickens out of Whitney. It was the only way Matt figured they could get her to quit.

Adkins said he didn't understand why they didn't just go to the police and turn in dirt like Elroy. But they told him they didn't want Whitney in trouble.

So Adkins said he would help. He'd get a disguise and meet them where they planned, at Lambeth Park just after eight. Matt and Mike had watched Whitney leave Elroy's a couple nights in a row, a rolled-up grocery bag in her hand, as if she were carrying a bag of penny candy. She always walked through the park, so that's where they waited for her—in the bushes beside the sidewalk, east of the wading pool.

"I don't know if I can keep from laughing," Mike said.

Matt gave him an elbow. "This is serious," he said.

When Whitney came bicycling along the path, Adkins stepped out and grabbed her handlebars. "Police," he said. "What's in the bag?"

Mike about died laughing. Matt tried to shush him.

Whitney's eyes flashed like moons. "It's nothing," she said. "Cookies—um—cookies is all."

"Sure," he said. "Don't be lying to me, young lady."

Then Whitney did something wild. She slung the bike at Adkins and tried to take off. But her foot caught over the bar and she tripped and fell in the grass, the bag beneath her, hidden.

"You better give it up, girl," Adkins said, in a real low voice. "Your hide's already in hot water."

Whitney's whole body was shaking. "It's just something I do for this guy," she said. "He just gave me a job, see. I deliver stuff. I don't know what. I just take it where he says."

Adkins grabbed the bag. "Tell it to the judge."

Matt rolled his eyes. Adkins made it sound so much like TV.

"Looks like you and I go for a little ride," he said, tossing the bag in his hand. "Cookies is it?"

"I don't know," she kept telling him. "Really, this guy pays me for taking it." She held both hands up to her face as she stood slowly.

"You know one of the kids you bring this to is dead?"

Mike just about lost it on that one. "Where'd that come from?" he whispered.

Matt figured Adkins must be making it up as he went.

"The kid fingered you before he died—"

"He sounds like such a jerk," Mike said. "Why isn't he more like Colombo?"

No one saw Elroy come up, but before they knew it he'd hit Adkins—slammed him over the head with something loose and hard, like a rock in the end of sock—and Adkins went down, cold.

"Who is this guy anyway?" Elroy said, looking around. "You know this guy? Who is he? What happened?"

Elroy squeezed Whitney's arm so hard that Matt knew it hurt her. "He said he was a cop—" she said.

"He's no cop." Elroy let go of her arm, fell to his knees, and searched through Adkins' pockets until he found his billfold. "Told you he's no cop," Elroy said, tossing it away.

"He said he was," Whitney told him.

"Look at this guy's face," he said. "You don't recognize him, do you? Look good."

Whitney stared down at Adkins. Matt figured it was over now, that she'd recognize him right away. She looked closely, then her eyes dropped.

"I don't know him," she said.

"Well, he knows *you*," Elroy snarled. "Look closer."

Whitney was almost crying. Fear strangled her voice when she blurted. "It's a teacher. I know him. It's a teacher."

"A teacher?" he said. "You're done, you know—and so am I. Let's get out of here."

"I'm going home," she said. "My bicycle—"

"No, you're not, girl," Elroy said. "You're coming with me now. We've got to leave." He took her arm again and jerked her around.

"Now what?" Mike said.

Everything they'd planned had turned out bad. Adkins lay there bleeding, Elroy was dragging Whitney off. Everything was much, much worse than it was supposed to be. They had meant to do right, he thought, but the bad guys were winning. Adkins said he shouldn't just quit on somebody like Whitney—it wasn't what God wanted him to do. So where was God now? Where?

You're in charge of everything, Lord, every moment we live. You've created us—and our world. You've given us blessings. You've given us your Son. Help us never to forget you are Lord of all the earth. Amen.

MEDITATION 56
GREATNESS

Psalm 145:1-7

Today Michael Jordan "owns" basketball. He accelerates as if he were born with a hidden, reusable fuse; and he's got a vertical jump that flies right off the charts. Any of a dozen of his moves on a given night replay on late sports shows across the continent. With or without the ball, Michael Jordan's a magician, a franchise. His greatness lies in his simply stupendous athletic ability.

* * * * * *

My kids can't believe it when I sing along with the Beach Boys. They think their father is way too old to appreciate the sweet floating sound of such California crooning. Besides, they think their dad the teacher isn't supposed to swoon over beach parties and Hollywood hot rods. But I can't help it—twenty years ago I knew every last word the Beach Boys recorded. The summer-like spells their songs cast make their music great. They keep people singing along—even when they're forty or more.

* * * * * *

Some nights when we watch Bill Cosby shape his face in sorry twists, members of my family all break out laughing at once. Cosby's always been a wonderful comedian, but his show is really great. And it stays popular even though it doesn't have murders and car chases and nudity like many other popular shows do. What makes Cosby great is that we see ourselves in his silly face.

* * * * * *

Beloved, a novel by Toni Morrison, is the best book I've read in the last year. When I finished it, I could hardly move. In this book, Denver, a young mother, risks absolutely everything to keep her children from the slavery that she's just left, now that the Civil War is over. Slowly, the reader comes to know Denver and through her to see the real horror of slavery. What's great about *Beloved* is the way it makes you understand slavery—and yet gives you hope that life is still somehow worthwhile.

* * * * * *

PSALMS 145 & 150

Mother Teresa has given her life to poor and desolate people, especially the children of India. Day after day she fights hopelessness, malnutrition, and broken souls. She won't give up, not even when governments throw in the towel. Mother Teresa's greatness lies in her tenacious compassion.

* * * * * *

It's not hard to recognize greatness—that quality that pushes individual human beings over the heads of the crowd. Of course, not all great people are alike: Cosby is a comedian, Toni Morrison a writer, and Mother Teresa a humanitarian. Mother Teresa probably couldn't stuff a basketball like Michael Jordan can, even when she was nineteen. And Toni Morrison probably can't paint on a scowl like Cosby can. The Beach Boys will never be Boy Scouts, much less a bunch of Mother Teresas.

In each case, greatness is still only human. Fifty years from now, Cosby's wonderful face will be gone. Michael Jordan's knees will be sawdust, and the Beach Boys' voices will sound like four straw brooms on concrete. Greatness doesn't last.

Except God's. "Great is the Lord and most worthy of praise," David says; "his greatness no one can fathom." God's greatness soars so much higher than Michael Jordan's that they aren't even on the same court.

And his greatness is defined in this: he loves his people—us—and he has, forever and ever. His greatness is magnificent goodness. Believe me, no one else can touch him.

Dear Lord, help us to appreciate your greatness, to understand that your power and glory will last forever and ever. Amen.

UNSTOPPABLE PRAISE

....

Psalm 145:9-21

I don't use the word *miracle* easily, but what the Dodgers did to the Oakland A's in the 1988 World Series has to be judged with the great upsets of all times—almost a miracle.

Only Band-Aids and a megadose of spirit kept the no-names together. Baseball pundits figured Oakland's musclemen to be one of the great teams of all baseball history. Yet the Dodgers took the A's in five, as if they were squaring off against a bunch of local yokels swinging straws.

I watched the opening game and thereby witnessed one of the great moments of baseball history: a half-crippled Kirk Gibson limped up to the plate in the ninth inning, pulled a full count, and then slammed Dennis Eckersley's slider right out of the park.

That home run exploded out of sheer human will rolled up into whatever strength Gibson could muster, and as he pumped his way around second, his bad knees barely keeping him up, I nearly bawled.

It was Gibson's only time at bat in all five games, but I'm sure I'm not the only one who believes that Gibson's opening-game blast determined the outcome of the series.

I was watching the game alone. My wife was in another room, but after I saw Gibson round the bases, I told her she had to watch. "This is incredible," I yelled. "The guy can barely walk, and he just parked one to win the first game. You got to see this." My wife's far less a fan than I am, but she came in and watched the replay while I blurted out the whole story, praising Gibson for his heroics.

Why did I make her watch the replay? Why did I chase her away from whatever she was doing and pull her to the TV?

I think it's because when we see or experience something really great, we *have to* praise it. We just have to tell someone. There's such sweet joy in telling somebody, "That was incredible." Even if I'd been home alone that night, I bet I would have talked out loud. I swear it. It had to come out.

In *Reflections on the Psalms*, C. S. Lewis claims that "we delight to praise what we enjoy because praise not merely expresses but completes the enjoyment; it is its appointed consummation."

Psalms 145 and 150 are great psalms of praise. They explode out of David's great joy. David knows that God's been with him through thick and thin, and he knows God loves him in spite of everything. He can't help but praise God. It's almost instinct. His joy will not be complete until he praises God.

"For God so loved the world that he gave his one and only Son, that whoever believes in him shall not perish but have eternal life."

Praise be! Incredible! Just awesome! Wow!

....

Fill us with your Spirit, Lord. Help us to know that we are your people and that you brought your Son into this world to die for us. Excite us with what you've done. Give us joy and let us praise your name forever. Amen.

DANCING BEFORE THE LORD

....

Psalm 150

One night almost thirty years ago, when my parents weren't home, my sister taught me how to twist like Chubby Checker.

"It's like you just got out of the bathtub," she said, "and you're drying off your rear end with a towel." She grabbed a towel from the bathroom and held one end in her right hand, strapped it around her behind, and grabbed the other end in her left. I flipped on the record. "Let's twist again, like we did last summer—pah! pah!"—out came Chubby's voice.

"Like this," she said, and she started jerking that towel around her bottom in perfect time to the music. "It's easy," she told me, throwing away the towel. "Try it."

We were hidden away upstairs—only my sister and me.

Okay, I admit it, it was fun. In a couple of minutes we started goofing around, lifting a foot off the floor while we were wiggling, or stooping down low like Chubby himself. " 'Round and around and up and a down we go—"

Part of the reason I liked it was because I was sure it was naughty. If my parents would have caught us wiggling to Chubby Checker right there in our house, they would have worn down our behinds with more than towels. I was raised in a home in which dancing was thought to be an activity meant only for bad kids, not fit exercise for onward Christian soldiers.

So today, I still have trouble with Psalm 150: "praise him with tambourine and dancing." I'll buy the tambourine any day, but dancing? It seems similar to saying, "Bless the Lord with booze."

I know people today who use a verse like this one to argue that we should be dancing in church. I think the theory is okay, although I admit that I'm not anxious to watch some choir director break into a Christian hokey-pokey. But that's not to say it couldn't be done.

David was quite a dancer, especially if we believe his wife Michal. When David and his men brought the ark back to Jerusalem, he danced up such a frenzy that Michal told him he behaved like a jerk. "You're quite the king," she told him, "stripping yourself in front of all the slave girls like some macho clod."

But if you read that story carefully, you'll see that Michal's concern for her husband isn't so super-righteous. Michal never merits much of God's blessing in David's story.

I suppose anything we do can turn into sin—body checks, slam dunks, bike races, gunning for tests, even going to church, if it is done for the wrong reason. A preacher can sin preaching a sermon if all he wants to do is charm an audience.

The day may come when I'll go to church and get up and dance with everybody else. Stranger things have happened. But for now, what I like about "praising the Lord with dancing" is the idea that everything we do—all our cellos and kazoos, our fox trots and our corner kicks, our math tests and our slumber parties—every last thing we do, in fact, can bring praise to the God who loved us, even when we didn't love him.

God is Lord of all of life. And I like what the psalmist says here in this last great psalm: in everything you do, praise the Lord God Almighty, King and Creator of the universe.

In everything. Even twisting with Chubby Checker.

In all we do, in every last thing, help us to see ourselves as your children, your people, your loved ones. Give us the ability to work for you in this world—in whatever we do, day in and day out. Amen.

WHAT ABOUT THE WHITE SPACE?

....

Psalm 13

Put yourself in a director's chair, slap on a black beret, and put a candy cigarette into the fancy brass holder, one of those with curly ends. Play the part.

You're the director, and standing right before you are some of the greatest actors and actresses in the country—Susan Sarandon, Meryl Streep, Dustin Hoffman, and Kevin Costner. Hoffman is playing David in a film about David's life. His lines today include Psalm 13.

Hoffman looks at you for help. "I can't figure this out," he says. "How do I do it?"

The problem is the white space. He says he's got no trouble at all with the anger and the doubt in the first four verses. He can rant and rage and knock over golden goblets. He doesn't have any problem with verses 5 and 6 either. He can settle down and let a long, winsome smile stretch over his face in a dream of peace.

"But what do I do in the white space?" he asks.

You're not sure what he means. "I don't understand," you tell him.

"Look at the lines," he says. "There's all this anger and doubt, all this fist-waving. And then all of a sudden—in the white space between verses 4 and 5—I change completely. From anger to praise—bang!—just like that. How do I do it?"

You look again at the script, stick the candy cigarette holder between your lips. He's right, of course. Hoffman's no rookie. The first four verses are full of anger: "How long, O Lord?"—he says it four times in a row, as if he's steamed at God for getting lost in all the misery. And then, in verse 5, his attitude suddenly changes: "But I trust in your unfailing love; my heart rejoices in your salvation."

What must he do in the white space? How must he act?

How do you answer him?

You look again and again at the text, and you remember what you know of the psalms.

What you've got to understand, you tell him, is that all the howling in the first four verses isn't aimed at an empty sky. Even when he's mad, David talks to God because he knows God is there. All the screaming, you say, is aimed at real ears.

David is always honest to God, and his honesty brings reward. David knows that this God who listens has listened before—and has acted before. That's why he praises God in the last two verses. He's sure, even when he doubts.

So you tell Dustin Hoffman to keep staring at one point all through the howling. Don't let your eyes wander around, you say, as if you don't know where he is. David's talking to someone, not to himself. Tell Hoffman to stare at God, as if he were there beside him—because David knows full well that he is.

Tell him to try that. That will make the change easier.

All one hundred fifty psalms are songs of praise. Even when they start in doubt or fear or real hurt, they end in praise, because all the song writers know that the great I AM exists now and forever, and that he will, strangely enough, love them. That's his promise.

Praise be to God. Honestly.

Thank you for the psalms, Lord. We can feel our own pulse beating in what they bring to you. Help us to find ourselves in the songs your people have sung for centuries. Help us praise—as David did—every day. In Jesus' name, Amen.

PSALMS 145 & 150

HONESTY XII

Park lights ran in long strings along the sidewalks, but Elroy, grabbing Whitney's arm, stayed in the darkness.

"He's takin' her away," Mike said. "He's going to kidnap her. I just know it—"

Matt came out from behind the bushes. Adkins was slowly picking himself up, holding his head. There was blood all right.

"It's our last chance," he said to Mike. "You help Adkins. I got to do something."

Matt slipped off his shoes in the grass and took off running, as quietly as he could, after Elroy and Whitney. He could hear in Elroy's growling that Whitney was in trouble. He had one hand on her, the other on the bag. Matt knew the crumb cared more for the bag than he did for Whitney. So maybe if he could grab the bag, Whitney could take off.

The grass felt soft and wet on his toes. It was his only chance. He took off in long quiet steps until he was right behind them. In full stride Matt grabbed the bag out of Elroy's hands, then raced off into the darkness, Elroy yelling and swearing behind him, hot on his trail.

Matt knew the park much better than Elroy did. At the bandstand he circled left, trying to stay out of the lights. His legs felt like feathers beneath him. He was running like the wind, like he never had before. He flew up behind the bushes around the jungle gym, glancing back to make sure Elroy was still coming.

The deepest darkness was at the creek bank, up against the houses at the east end of the park. So Matt headed in that direction, his breath coming harder, scared but still sure that he could outrun the Burger Barn man. He sprinted through the rim of lights along the sidewalk, headed down to the creek and up the bank on the other side. If he could get to the houses, Matt thought, he could lose Elroy for sure. He had nothing to lose if somebody called the cops because of all the commotion. Not now.

Elroy stopped screaming once he got close to the houses, but Matt didn't slow down. He galloped down into the grass and jumped the creek, then climbed up the bank with the bag in his teeth, and vaulted the park fence into somebody's backyard. Matt couldn't hear Elroy anymore, but he wasn't taking any chances. He ran out the side gate and took a sharp left through the front lawns of two houses, then hid behind a garage.

When he looked back, there was no Elroy.

Matt waited for what seemed like hours, but nothing moved. He was safe. If only Whitney took off, he thought.

He climbed out slowly and stayed close to the houses as he made his way slowly back into the park by way of the long grass in the creek.

"Matt," someone whispered, "is that you?"

It was Whitney all right, right beneath the bridge. She had her face in her hands. He was glad she was free, but he was mad too. "It's me, all right," he said. "Watch this." He opened the bag and dumped all the stuff right into the creek. "It's gone—the whole stinking mess."

"I'm sorry," she said.

"Where is your buddy?" he asked her.

"I ran once you grabbed the bag. He was going to take me with him, he said—"

"It's okay." Even in the darkness he could see the streaks down her face. "He's gone—long gone. He's in hot water."

"He would have hurt you," she said. "You know that?"

"I didn't plan on getting caught," Matt said.

She looked up to the sky, as if to hold in tears. "Why did you help?" she said. "I didn't even care—"

"Stupid Adkins," he said. "He's the guy that cares. He said I couldn't just write you off. He said you needed me and that I better help you. You should have heard him read me out."

"Why?"

Matt knew why of course, but he didn't know how to say it. "Because he says it's right is all—how do I know?"

"So why did you do it—for Adkins?"

"You needed me," he said. "He was right."

Whitney pulled her fingers through her hair. "I'll never forget what you did," she told him. "I was so scared. I'm sorry."

Matt took Whitney's hand and walked with her through the darkness toward Mike and Adkins. Never in his life had Matt felt quite what he felt just then. He'd done something very important, something more important and good than he'd ever, ever done before. Whitney was here now, away from the jerk. For a minute, he almost felt like crying, but instead he prayed—just a word or so, that's all.

Not even out loud. Just thanks, thanks for everything. It came up honestly, and it felt good. It felt very, very good.

Make our prayers honest and true, Lord. Open up our hearts to see your face and to feel your continuing presence in our lives. Help us to keep talking to you, to keep ourselves close to your power and strength and love. Amen.